101 ESSENTIAL LISTS
ON ASSESSMENT

101 ESSENTIAL LISTS SERIES

101 ESSENTIAL LISTS
ON ASSESSMENT

Tabatha Rayment

continuum
LONDON • NEW YORK

Continuum International Publishing Group
The Tower Building   80 Maiden Lane
11 York Road   Suite 704
London   New York
SE1 7NX   NY 10038

www.continuumbooks.com

British Library Cataloguing-in-Publication Data
A catalogue record for this book is available from the British Library.

ISBN: 0-8264-8867-6 (paperback)

Library of Congress Cataloguing-in-Publication Data
A catalog record for this book is available from the Library of Congress.

Typeset by YHT Ltd
Printed and bound in Great Britain by Ashford Colour Press Ltd,
Gosport, Hampshire

CONTENTS

INTRODUCTION

As all teachers know, assessment is a continuous, cyclical process. Assessing academic progress has been one of the key responsibilities of any professional educator.

However, how does any teacher or assessor know what to look for?

Assessment comes in many forms: from marking exercise books, to judging athletic ability, from a performance in drama, to student behaviour in class. More importantly, just how necessary is assessment to the learning process? This book contains 101 essential lists to help and advise when dealing with assessment. From using formative assessment to determine what is known, to continuously self-assessing teaching progress, these lists are easy to follow and provide effective strategies when put into practice.

Tabatha Rayment
Leicester 2006

Explaining Assessment

LIST 1 What is assessment?

Assessment is the process whereby evidence is obtained through the outcome of specific questioning such as tests and surveys, and used to determine results based on the findings of such methods. These may also define the status or value of an event, thing or person's abilities based on performance or importance.

However, in an educational context, assessment is:

- A method of enquiry to determine the extent of learning.
- A method to acquire and collect essential feedback.
- The process of evaluating students within an educational context.
- The process of documenting knowledge, skills, attitude and beliefs.
- An essential teaching approach and technique.
- A cyclical and continuous process to evaluate teaching and learning.
- A method to determine how best teaching and learning should continue.
- A diagnostic and evaluative tool.

Effective assessment

Not all assessment is useful and necessary. Being too draconian or over-analysing performance can have a negative effect on the student. In order to make the process a positive one, it is important to think about what you wish to achieve for yourself and the student during your evaluation.

Effective assessment

- ○ Evaluates the extent of learning taken place.
- ○ Is an essential part of the learning process for both teachers and learners.
- ○ Acts as a systematic process of obtaining evidence.
- ○ Promotes effective learning when used in the correct way.
- ○ Determines the next steps needed to continue the process of teaching and learning.
- ○ Offers positive ways to reaffirm talent, ability and understanding.
- ○ Has many purposes: it allows both teachers and learners to see levels of achievement and areas for improvement.
- ○ Takes many forms: e.g. it can be verbal, written, collaborative, personal and spontaneous among other variations, depending on the circumstances.
- ○ Assists teachers to deliver accurate and informative lessons and feedback.
- ○ Can be used to monitor social, academic and behavioural progress.

LIST 3

When is assessment most effective?

The following are essential golden rules for making sure that you get the best results out of evaluation and assessment techniques.

Assessment is the most effective when

- ○ Shared with the pupils involved, and, where appropriate, peers, other teachers, parents and carers.
- ○ Focused on specific areas of learning and individual progress.
- ○ Used to help pupils understand how to improve.
- ○ Clearly linked to targets and achievements.
- ○ It is honest, positive and appraising of achievement and effort.
- ○ It is concise not dismissive.
- ○ It is relative to the subject.
- ○ It recognizes progress and clearly explains how to improve.

Why is assessment important?

Although it is accepted that assessment is an essential part of effective teaching and learning, few of us ever stop to consider why.

Good-quality assessment is essential for the following reasons:

○ It allows teachers and learners to determine the standard of their work and consider how they might improve.
○ It helps teachers to plan effective lessons that take into account the individual needs of each student.
○ It allows monitoring of the quality of education being delivered.
○ It allows student progress to be monitored effectively to ensure targets are being met.
○ It can assist in the motivation of students.
○ It can help students make informed educational and career-based decisions.
○ It can assist in ensuring a good-quality curriculum is being delivered and maintained.
○ It can ensure the necessary resources and finances are being put to good use within the school.
○ It can help to determine that tests and assignments are relevant and helpful to the achievement process.

The impact of assessment

What does assessment actually do for the individual?

For the student

- Helps them become better monitors of, and involve them in, their own learning.
- Helps break down any possible feelings of anonymity, especially in large groups.
- Helps highlight any potential areas for concern and suggest positive changes to raise achievement.
- Shows that the teacher actively cares about the student's learning.
- Helps increase self-esteem and self-confidence – the student knows what they have achieved and can be proud of their abilities.

For the teacher

- Helps ensure that lesson plans, both long and short-term, are effective and appropriate.
- Ensures that teaching and learning strategies are proving to be effective.
- Heightens teacher/learner awareness and enforces positive relationships through the learning process.
- Improves relationships between teacher and student – shows the teacher is genuinely interested in how the student performs and achieves.

LIST 6
What Ofsted says about assessment

The Office for Standards in Education (Ofsted) was established under the Education (Schools) Act 1992 and takes responsibility for monitoring the standards of all schools, state and independent. It is committed to raising standards and ensuring the delivery of effective education.

○ Ofsted wants all schools to be aware of how assessment can assist in improving standards of learning and achievement.
○ The quality and use of ongoing assessment has been observed to be 'good' or 'better' in only 40 per cent of schools recently inspected.
○ Ofsted inspectors frequently judge new teachers' assessment skills to be poor or weak in comparison to their other skills.
○ The most commonly noted problem areas are:
   – poor quality of feedback given to pupils and their parents or guardians
   – insufficient guidance is given to encourage improvement
   – strengths and weaknesses are not described enough
   – marking is inconsistent or unconstructive
   – lack of ipsative* assessment
   – pupils are given few opportunities to reflect on comments
○ Suggestions to improve effective assessment:
   – improve the quality of focus on teaching and learning within the whole school
   – explain objectives and outcomes clearly before each lesson
   – link lessons and assessment strategies to National Standards
   – keep assessment consistent and appropriate
   – give students opportunities to evaluate their own work and actively engage in the assessment process
   – use formative assessment productively to ensure teaching and learning is effective and students' needs are being met
   – collaborate with other members of staff, education professionals and parents to ensure each individual's education is being supported

* *Ipsative assessment* is when progress is linked to assessment and used to improve performance – e.g. current achievements are compared with previous ones to determine the level of progression.

Positive Assessment | 2

LIST 7   Encouraging self-esteem

Assessment has a considerable impact on the self-esteem and self-confidence of any individual, teacher and learner. Assessment should *not* be about giving criticism or passing judgement. It should be used to highlight areas where an individual has succeeded and done well, and to encourage feelings of self-worth and achievement.

Positive effects

- Promotes a sense of achievement.
- Rewards goals and attainment.
- Encourages target setting and the desire to achieve more.
- Gives the learner a sense of worth.
- Shows areas for improvement and how to tackle problems optimistically.
- Puts learning into a bigger picture so learners can see their achievements as a whole.
- Reduces the risk of isolated learning or 'blind' learning – offers a positive reason behind a task or assignment.
- Promotes a good relationship between teachers and learners by showing a genuine interest in pupil achievement.
- Allows students to take responsibility for their learning.
- Encourages pupils' confidence in their skills.

Negative effects

- Can overemphasize failures or poor achievement.
- Can be potentially damaging if learners do not achieve as well as they had hoped.
- Can become too goal-orientated without rewarding previous achievements.
- When used too often or inappropriately, can become superficial.
- Can draw unwanted attention from peers.

- Can unintentionally promote comparison-making between peers.
- Summative, formal assessments can potentially reduce the bigger picture of learning by making it all about grades.
- Assessment for streaming can be damaging to a student's sense of ambition – low achievers can feel that there is no point in aiming high as they cannot achieve high rewards.

LIST 8 — A positive experience

Appraisal and encouragement are essential parts of assessment. However, when the assessment results turn out to be bad news for the student, how can you keep assessment positive?

○ Focus on what *has* been achieved, rather than what the pupil has failed at.

○ Always keep comments positive and encouraging, never criticize.

○ Take time to praise the student, even if it is only a small achievement.

○ Avoid cursory and unhelpful comments such as 'must try harder'; opt instead for more constructive and encouraging remarks such as: 'this work would benefit from ...'

○ Avoid generalizations; always link your assessment to specific areas of an individual's work.

○ Give realistic and helpful targets to help pupils to improve.

○ Avoid correcting every single mistake: this looks daunting for anyone, not just a student.

○ Offer pupils a chance to assess their own work and to suggest improvements of their own.

○ Use ipsative assessment to show areas that have been, or that need to be, improved on.

○ Written comments should follow the three-part rule with one part being praise and two parts being suggestions for improvement.

○ Take the time to involve students in their assessment and discuss results or ideas together.

LIST 9 Motivation

Assessment monitors levels of attainment, while motivation helps to give the individual the drive to achieve. How can good assessment assist in encouraging and motivating a learner?

○ Give credit where credit is due: praising current attainment and good work helps to improve levels of self-esteem and confidence in the learner.

○ Unbiased, target-focused assessment ensures that current skills are recognized while giving the individual something to aim towards, rather than merely gaining grades.

○ Good feedback promotes involvement and shows that the teacher is taking an active interest in the learner.

○ Rewarding achievement in the form of positive marking, gold stars or a simple 'well done' helps to enforce a sense of achievement and satisfaction in the learner.

○ Mistakes or problems can be clearly identified, allowing the student a chance to improve and expand on their skills.

○ Making learning a fun challenge encourages pupils to 'win'. The prize of achievement is the satisfaction in knowing you have accomplished something.

Giving encouragement

A happy student will be a hard-working student, or so the theory goes. No learner, not even an adult will want to put hard work into a project that does not do much for them personally, or leaves them without any sense of achievement. As a consequence, encouraging and motivating students is essential to ensure that they get the most out of the learning process, and you have a cheerful and attentive class.

○ Give frequent, positive and accessible feedback.
○ Ensure students feel involved and valued.
○ Provide opportunities for success.
○ Create a positive learning environment.
○ Suggest ways of approaching areas of difficulty, to encourage problem-solving and sustain interest.
○ Help students to find personal meaning in the material they learn.
○ Help pupils to see the bigger picture of education.
○ Explain the positive benefits of good education and achievement.
○ Make learning fun and enjoyable.
○ Consistently praise achievement.
○ Provide opportunities for students to take ownership of their learning.
○ Set clear rules for behaviour.
○ Use a variety of teaching styles and learning resources.
○ Ensure lessons are varied and stimulating.
○ Encourage other forms of learning such as extracurricular activities.
○ Value the students' contributions and opinions – be aware of every individual's needs.
○ Be a positive and enthusiastic teacher – never give up even when teaching 'difficult' or 'challenging' classes.
○ Be a positive role model.

Behaviour

Not all assessment is linked to attaining good grades; monitoring student behaviour is also an important part of classroom assessment. It would be foolish to think that any student can learn effectively in an environment that lacks order or discipline.

Positive learning can only take place in a positive atmosphere, and behaviour management should be taken just as seriously (if not more so) as planning, delivery and marking.

To promote good behaviour in the classroom, assessment can be used to:

❍ Ensure all students are working and behaving in an acceptable way.
❍ Ensure that language use and attitude is of an acceptable standard.
❍ Check that achievement levels are not being affected by poor behaviour.

Assessment of behaviour can be implemented in the following ways:

❍ Setting and defining goals and targets.
❍ Tally charts displayed in the classroom (merits/stars/reward tokens or smiley charts, etc.).
❍ Openly encouraging and praising good behaviour.
❍ Seating plans to ensure that students are in the optimum working environment.
❍ Regular interaction between student and teacher to discuss behaviour and review targets.
❍ Individual Education Plans (IEPs) or Individual Behaviour Plans (IBPs) to discuss targets and implement strategies focusing on achievement.
❍ Modelling and prompting of desired behaviour.
❍ Rewarding acceptable behaviour immediately, systematically and fairly.
❍ Home/School diaries completed by teachers, students and parents focusing on good behaviour.
❍ Time-outs or isolation strategies if necessary to return the focus to good behaviour and achievement.

Individual Behaviour Plans

Students who consistently exhibit worrying or unwanted behaviour may benefit from the use of an Individual Behaviour Plan (IBP). These allow teachers to work together with the students to assess and reduce behavioural issues, and encourage them to take responsibility for their own actions.

The contents of an IBP can include:

Improving attendance and punctuality

- ○ Attends school every day
- ○ Good time-keeping skills: arrives at school and for lessons on time
- ○ Follows the timetable set for them

On-task behaviour in lessons

- ○ Is on-task during the lesson
- ○ Enters the classroom sensibly and starts work promptly
- ○ Works without supervision and concentrates on the task
- ○ Completes targets set for them during the lesson
- ○ Completes all homework or additional class activities on time
- ○ Shares equipment and resources with others if necessary

Attention and concentration skills

- ○ Listens to teacher instructions
- ○ Raise their hands if they wish to speak
- ○ Does not interrupt the teacher or other students
- ○ Listens to the opinions of other students without interrupting
- ○ Remains focused during oral tasks
- ○ Remains seated where expected unless asked to move

Reducing attention-seeking or rude behaviour

- ○ Acts sensibly and maturely both in class and around the school
- ○ Does not shout out or act inappropriately
- ○ Does not use rude or offensive language in class or around the school
- ○ Follows instructions without arguing or debating

- Does not act in an inappropriate, disruptive or dangerous way
- Is polite and considerate to others around the school
- Does not threaten other pupils either physically or verbally
- Learns to control their temper and remain calm at all times when in the school

Organizational and motivational skills

- Arrives for the lesson with the correct equipment
- Is appropriately dressed in the school uniform
- Ensures all exercise books are brought to school as required
- Completes all homework by the required time and to a good standard
- Works towards the expected standards of the class
- Asks sensibly for help if it is needed
- Takes an interest in their own learning

Improving self-esteem

- Accepts praise from teachers, other adults and their peers
- Accepts guidance and advice when offered
- Has a positive personal attitude
- Seeks to cooperate, and make friends with, others
- Is proud of their own achievements

Assessment and the National Curriculum

3

 LIST 13 | **Attainment targets and National Curriculum levels**

Every teacher in a UK maintained school is familiar with the National Curriculum, and its impact on teaching and learning. From the initial stages of planning a lesson to the recorded assessment of each student's progress, the National Curriculum provides a framework that dictates pupil performance across the school.

○ Pupil achievement of National Curriculum attainment target levels will depend largely on the intake of the school and the ability of the class.
○ In all National Curriculum subjects, except Citizenship, the attainment targets consist of eight level descriptors.
○ Each level descriptor increases in difficulty, with an extra descriptor for outstanding achievement over Level 8.
○ The level descriptors are used to provide a solid basis for judging pupil performance at the end of Key Stages 1, 2 and 3.
○ At Key Stages 4 and 5, students are assessed by means of national qualifications.

The following table shows how pupils are separated into Key Stage groups according to age:

	Key Stage 1	Key Stage 2	Key Stage 3	Key Stage 4
Age	5–7	7–11	11–14	14–16
Year Groups	1–2	3–6	7–9	10–11

The National Curriculum dictates what levels the majority of pupils are expected to reach by the end of each Key Stage. This sets clear targets for each age range and allows teachers to plan lessons accordingly.

The following table shows these expected levels for each Key Stage:

Range of levels within which the great majority of pupils are expected to work		Expected attainment for the majority of pupils at the end of the key stage.	
Key stage 1	1–3	At age 7	2
Key stage 2	2–5	At age 11	4
Key stage 3	3–7	At age 14	5/6

Reproduced from *The National Curriculum Handbook for secondary teachers in England*, 1999

Early years

Foundation Stage

○ Initial assessment begins in the Foundation Stage, when the child reaches the age of 3, and continues until the end of the reception year – the year they turn 5.

○ Not all children will be a part of Foundation Stage assessment, as some children stay at home until they reach school age.

○ Children are not expected to take any tests or exams at this age; the Foundation Stage profile is built and added to over the year.

○ The Foundation Stage profile is based around six areas of learning:
  - personal, social and emotional development
  - communication, language and literacy
  - mathematical development
  - knowledge and understanding of the world
  - physical development
  - creative development

○ These six areas form the basis of Early Learning goals, which all children are expected to achieve and, where possible, go beyond.

○ The Early Learning goals are a set of 13 assessment scales, which are divided into 9 points.

○ Foundation Stage profiles must be completed for each child at the end of their foundation stage, at least 4 weeks before the summer term ends.

Key Stage 1

○ By the age of 5, a child is expected to have begun Key Stage 1.

○ At the end of Key Stage 1 the child is usually aged 7, although some children may be slightly older or younger.

○ At the end of Key Stage 1, every child is expected to take a range of tests and tasks according to their level of ability in English and Mathematics.

○ The Key Stage 1 English tests comprise:
  - Reading task (levels 1–2)
  - Reading test (level 2)
  - Reading test (level 3)
  - Writing tasks (levels 1–3), which comprise:
    - longer task

- – shorter task
- – spelling test
- – handwriting judgement
○ The Key Stage 1 Mathematics test comprises:
  - – Mathematics task (level 1)
  - – Mathematics test (level 2)
  - – Mathematics test (level 3)
○ For more able pupils there are four English and three Mathematics tests available.
○ These additional tests are designed to challenge and motivate more able pupils and encourage a wider range of thinking and learning.

Middle years

Key Stage 2

○ Key Stage 2 begins at the start of Year 3 (age 7) and finishes at the end of Year 6 (age 11).

○ At the end of Key Stage 2, all children are formally assessed in 3 core subjects: English, Mathematics and Science.

○ At 11 years old, most children are expected to be working at Level 4.

○ At the end of Key Stage 2, children are required to take the following tests:
  – Reading test (levels 3–5)
  – Writing test (levels 3–5)
  – Spelling test (levels 3–5)
  – Mathematics test A (levels 3–5)
  – Mathematics test B (levels 3–5)
  – Mental mathematics (levels 3–5)
  – Science test A (levels 3–5)
  – Science test B (levels 3–5)

○ There are optional tests available for the more able students to challenge their ability and encourage motivation. They are not sufficient on their own to provide any indicative results or achievement level.

○ Pupils who do not manage to achieve level 4 in English and Mathematics at Key Stage 2 are eligible to take the Year 7 Progress Tests.

Secondary

Key Stage 3

○ Key Stage 3 begins at the start of Year 7 (age 11) and finishes at the end of Year 9 (age 14).

○ At the end of Key Stage 3 most students should be working at levels of 5–6.

○ Providing that the student is working at a specific level, at the end of Key Stage 3 he or she will be assessed by the statutory Key Stage 3 tests in English, Mathematics and Science.

○ The required levels for these tests are:
English – levels 4–7
Mathematics – levels 3–8
Science – levels 3–7

○ Pupil progress can be monitored through the optional Year 7 and 8 Progress Tests. These are helpful to ensure pupils are working towards desired targets across the years.

○ The breakdown for the Key Stage 3 compulsory tests is as follows:

English
– Reading paper (levels 4–7)
– Writing paper (levels 4–7)
– Shakespeare paper (levels 4-7)

Mathematics
– Paper 1 (levels 3–5; 4–6; 5–7 and 6–8)
– Paper 2 (levels 3–5, 4–6, 5–7 and 6–8)
– Mental mathematics test A (for use with levels 4–6; 5–7 and 6–8)
– Mental mathematics test B (for use with levels 4–6; 5–7 and 6–8)
– Mental mathematics test C (for use with levels 3–5)

Science
– Paper 1 (levels 3–6 and 5–7)
– Paper 2 (levels 3–6 and 5–7)

○ At the end of Key Stage 3 (age 14) all students are required to move towards taking their GCSEs.

Key Stage 4

○ Key Stage 4 begins at the start of Year 10 (age 14) and finishes at the end of Year 11 (age 16).

○ During Key Stage 4, students are expected to be making informed choices for their futures and at the end of the Key Stage they will be assessed by QCA examinations.

○ Secondary education in England and Wales follows the National Curriculum structure up until the end of Year 11. As of September 2004 the following subjects are compulsory at Key Stage 4.

Core subjects
– English
– Mathematics
– Science
– Physical Education
– Information and Communication Technology
– Citizenship

Other compulsory subjects
– Sex education
– Careers education
– Work-related learning
– Religious education

L I S T 17   GCSEs

The structure of secondary education is continuously changing, with the UK government focusing on how best to address the needs of today's students. At the end of Key Stage 4, all students are required to take exams to gain their General Certificate of Secondary Education (GCSEs) in the compulsory core subjects: English, Mathematics and Science.

○ Information and Communication Technology (ICT), Physical Education and Citizenship are compulsory subjects and must be followed; but not all schools will require students to work towards gaining a qualification in these areas.
○ From September 2004, the Arts, the Humanities, Design and Technology and Modern Foreign Languages were made Entitlement Areas and are no longer compulsory at Key Stage 4. However, all schools must provide these courses for students who wish to follow them.
○ Vocational subjects must also be available for study.
○ From 2006 all students will be required to take Science as a compulsory subject; however the requirements will change, giving the students a chance to achieve a double award GCSE.
○ For some students, the full curriculum might not be appropriate for maximizing a student's learning. In these cases a school may disapply. However, this application may only be granted after the student has had a careers interview, and only if the route of learning is seen to be a considerable improvement on the National Curriculum.
○ The GCSEs are formally graded by an external assessor and given a grade from A* to G.
○ A grade of A* to C is counted as a successful pass result.
○ Students will be given a chance to experience GCSE exam conditions through mock exam periods usually from November to February depending on the school and department policy.

Post 16

In the UK, compulsory education stops at the end of Year 11 (age 16) and students are given the choice as to whether they wish to continue their studies in Further Education.

There are many different routes of study available to students at this age, and it is often during Further Education that a student may make important choices that can affect their career paths later in life.

○ FE may take place in a sixth-form college, a further education college or a higher education institution.
○ Levels of FE study include: Further GCSE study, A Level, NVQ, City and Guilds and BTEC, Access and Recreational courses, plus others.
○ After completing courses in FE, some students will go on to continue their education even further into Higher Education at a university or other HE provider.
○ FE provides a stepping stone to many future career decisions and it is essential that all students be given guidance and advice to ensure they make the most of their FE studies.
○ All students should be offered clear and continuous careers guidance and support, particularly when choosing their FE subjects and when they are nearing the end of their study route.
○ One of the most popular routes of FE is to study Advanced (A) Levels. These can be put into two categories:
  – GCE AS/A Levels
  – VCE A Levels

GCE AS/A2 Levels

An academic GCE AS/A Level is the most popular choice among students entering FE. A Levels expand on some areas that have been touched upon in GCSE but require advanced thinking and deeper critical/analytical skills. More time can be spent on an A Level subject than on a GCSE, thus the student has the chance to learn much more and at a higher level.

- The GCE AS/A Levels are taken over either one or two years depending on whether the student wishes to achieve either a 1-year AS Level or a 2-year A Level.
- The Advanced Subsidiary (AS) is valued as half of a complete A Level qualification. It is also a qualification in its own right.
- It has three units that total 50 per cent of a full A Level. It is assessed to the same standard and levels expected from a student halfway through an A Level course.
- On successful completion of an AS Level subject, students can decide if they wish to continue their studies in this area and go on to take an A2 qualification. Successful completion of AS and A2 indicates that a student can be awarded a full A Level qualification.
- The A2 has three units that are assessed at the standards expected from a student at the end of an A Level course.
- Most AS and A2 units are assessed by an examination, although some may be assessed by coursework. In the majority of A Levels, coursework accounts for 20–30 per cent of the final mark.
- AS Levels cover less demanding material than A2s. In an A2 students will be given the opportunity to expand their knowledge and study the subject in-depth.

L I S T 20   VCE A Levels

A VCE is similar to a GCE A Level, but it is not considered to be so academic-focused. Students have the chance to learn technical or vocational skills that GCEs do not always offer. The high standard of learning is the same as that of a GCE.

○ VCEs are A Levels that allow students to expand their skills and knowledge in the same way as GCEs, but are considered to be less 'academic' and more 'hands on'. For this reason they are known as Vocational A Levels.

○ From September 2005, the VCEs have been restructured to follow the GCE AS/A2 format. A complete VCE is constructed of 12 units. An AS VCE has 6 units and is assessed to the standard expected from a student halfway through an A Level course.

○ There are four qualifications available through the VCE A Level route:

Advanced Subsidiary General Certificate of Education
3 × AS units: 1 externally assessed, 2 internally assessed. Graded A–E.

Advanced Subsidiary General Certificate of Education (double award)
6 × AS units: 2 externally assessed, 4 internally assessed. Graded AA, AB–EE.

Advanced General Certificate of Education
Six units (3 × AS units + 3 × A2 units): 2 externally assessed, 4 internally assessed. Graded A–E.

Advanced General Certificate of Education (double award)
Twelve units (6 × AS units + 6 × A2 units): 4 externally assessed, 8 internally assessed. Graded AA, AB–EE.
N.B. the internal and external assessment criteria are a guide only and may be open to change depending on the ability of the student or the subject studied.

○ Although the number of A Levels a student may study varies, it is usual to study four AS Levels in the first year and drop down to three A Levels in the second year, although some students do continue with their fourth subject. Most universities stipulate the need for a minimum of three A Levels in order to be accepted on a degree course, with some also asking for a fourth AS Level.

Pros and cons of A Levels

Pros

○ A Levels give students valuable experience of learning at a higher level and often encourage them to continue their education at university or through training courses.
○ A Levels allow students to pursue subjects they genuinely like and do well in.
○ The more relaxed atmosphere in FE means the student can feel more comfortable in a learning environment.
○ A Levels give the student a chance to expand on their skills and put them more in control of their learning.

Cons

○ Some students do not give as much thought as they should to how the qualification will help them in later life and merely study subjects they like or are good at.
○ Not all students who did well in a subject at GCSE level will continue their high attainment levels in A Level subjects due to the difficulty of some subjects.
○ Students who suffer from poor motivational skills often find they struggle with the workload that A Levels present.
○ A Level courses can be quite intensive and some students find it hard to cope with the pressures and expectations of Higher Learning.

Assessment and Learning | 4

Although assessment can take many forms, it is useful to separate each process into one of two main categories: Formative or Summative. It is important to be aware that these are not mutually exclusive, and many findings will be implemented in all stages and areas of assessment. You should also be aware of *ipsative assessment*. This focuses on how a learner's performance and achievements can be compared with earlier performances and achievements to see if any improvement has been made.

The following lists explain the two main types and how you might use them in the classroom.

Formative assessment – assessment for learning

This is the most common and frequently used form of assessment within the classroom and school. Often, teachers do not even realize they are using it, as it is an integral part of effective teaching and learning.

- Formative Assessment *informs* the learning.
- Happens continuously in a classroom environment.
- Involves both teacher and learner in a process of continual review and consideration regarding levels of progress.
- Provides constructive and encouraging feedback, allowing individuals to take responsibility for their own learning – e.g. the teacher gives the students suggestions on how they might improve their essay, and the students take these suggestions into consideration and implement them in their work.
- Allows lesson plans to be assessed and adjusted as necessary, making teachers instantly aware of any potential problems or areas of difficulty.
- Allows a teacher to plan lessons in line with their pupils' abilities.
- Is an exceptional asset to maintain effective and high-quality teaching standards.
- Can be oral or written feedback.
- May take the form of ipsative assessment.

Formative examples

Formative Assessment is used on a daily basis. It provides the students with the necessary guidance and information they need to progress in their learning. Teachers who do not use formative assessment while they teach are, quite simply, not performing as well as they should be.

On a day-to-day basis, formative assessment is used by:

○ Checking to see if the whole class is sure about what has been asked of them.
○ Engaging students through direct or 'hands-up' questioning.
○ Walking around the classroom to monitor students' progress.
○ Giving oral feedback to an individual or group, suggesting how they might improve on their class work.
○ The teacher offers suggestions on how students might improve their work.
○ The teacher guides a student or whole class through a task through modelling in their teaching.
○ Conscientious and up-to-date marking of work by pupils.
○ Openly praising good work done in class (e.g. a student paints a good picture in Art class and the teacher recognizes this achievement).
○ A student is reprimanded for poor behaviour in the playground.
○ A teacher takes time to ask how a student is feeling – shows an interest in the student as a person not just as a learner.

Things to be aware of

Although there is no doubt that Formative Assessment is an essential part of teaching and learning, make sure you use it appropriately and wisely.

The negative points of this Formative process are:

○ Danger of being too ad hoc (impulsive or improvised), and may not always provide an accurate degree of reliable objectivity.
○ Can be damaging to pupils' self-esteem if not used appropriately or sensitively.
○ Can be difficult to set and maintain rigid assessment standards if there is little or no 'paper work' to back it up.
○ Can lose meaning and impetus if used too often or incorrectly.
○ Can be too imposing if the teacher guides the class too often, or if the class relies on the teacher too much – 'spoon feeding'.
○ It can sometimes appear as if the teacher is favouring some students over others, especially if they commend or reprimand particular students more than others.

Summative assessment – assessment of learning

Summative Assessment is not used as often as Formative. This is a process that generally takes place at the end of a stage or task and summarizes the extent of learning that has taken place. It is a much more rigid form of assessment.

○ Summative assessment *sums up* the learning.
○ Is carried out by both subject teachers and a board of external examiners.
○ Is carried out at the end of a unit, Key Stage, year, or when the pupil is about to leave school.
○ Makes judgements regarding the pupil's progress and performance in relation to national standards.
○ Provides an overview of the pupils' attainment at the end of crucial stages in their education.
○ Takes the form of a monitored test or exam and is more commonly written than oral.
○ Can be used to monitor the performance of a whole school or group, not just an individual.

L I S T 26 — Assessment methods: normative and criterion

Summative assessment can be divided into two distinct assessment methods:

Normative assessment

- Concerned with national and local targets and Local Education Authority guidelines.
- Assesses the progress of a student in relation to others of the same peer group, age or ability.
- May involve ranking or scaling a pupil to help with streaming classes.
- May look at cross-school achievements to compare achievement in particular groups, subjects and years with local and national levels of attainment.

Criterion assessment

- Concerned with national examination and assessment bodies such as AQA, OCR, Edexcel, UCAS, etc.
- Is used in the assessment of vocational and academic qualifications.
- Determines if a student can carry out a specific task or activity within a particular situation or context.
- Results are given on a pass/fail, competent/not yet competent basis.
- Results are conclusive and not usually open to review.

Summative examples

Summative Assessment generally takes much longer to complete than Formative. The guidelines for Summative assessment are much more rigid and must be followed by all teachers. This process also involves much more paperwork and a more structured analysis of pupil achievement.

Examples include:

o Foundation Stage Assessments
o Standard Attainment Tests (SATs)
o General Certificate of Secondary Education (GCSE)
o General National Vocational Qualification (GNVQ)
o Advanced and Advanced Subsidiary Levels (A2 and AS Levels) and Advanced Extension Awards (for the top 10 per cent of A Level students)
o Key Skills tests
o Entry Level Qualifications
o National Vocational Qualifications and Vocational Qualifications (NVQs and VQs)
o Scottish Higher and Advanced Higher Qualifications
o Scottish Vocational Qualifications
o YELLIS/MIDYIS/ALIS, etc. (as part of the Curriculum, Evaluation and Management Centre at the University of Durham)

LIST 28 Things to be aware of

Summative Assessment can be easier to carry out than Formative, as teachers are given structured guidelines that inform them what, when and how to assess. However, this form also has its drawbacks.

○ Attainment levels are rigid and not usually open to review; the grade achieved is irrefutable.

○ Exams can only assess the pupil's performance on that day, regardless of performance levels outside of the exam situation.

○ Poor performance in an exam can make students' excellent performance over the year seem pointless, lowering their opinion of the education system.

○ Ranking or scaling pupils can be damaging to their self-esteem.

○ National exams carry great stress and pressure that can be overwhelming for many students, consequently affecting their performance.

○ Many students pin their future plans on gaining good grades in exams; a poor result can mean their goals are irreparably shattered.

○ School-based Summative assessment is time-consuming and means a lot of work for the teacher to ensure it is completed to a high standard.

○ Inexperienced teachers may find marking papers and tests difficult and may be too harsh or generous when awarding grades.

Assessment Strategies and Planning Lessons

LIST 29   Introducing WALT and WILF

Lesson objectives and outcomes should be shared with students at the beginning of every lesson. Using the acronyms WALT and WILF can help students to understand their targets.

WALT – We Are Learning To

- ○ Gives the teacher an opportunity to explain what the lesson means to the student – the Objective.
- ○ Gives the lesson an identifiable purpose or meaning.
- ○ Eliminates the danger of students learning 'dead' information or learning by rote.
- ○ Gives the students an active role in the lesson and in the learning process.
- ○ The students will be clear about what the lesson is offering and what skills or targets they can be expected to achieve.
- ○ Helps to link lessons over a set timescale with easily identifiable goals at the end.

WILF – What I'm Looking For

- ○ Gives the teacher an opportunity to explain the learning process – the Outcome.
- ○ Helps pupils understand the levels of assessment used and how their work will be assessed or graded.
- ○ Helps to give pupils clear targets to aim for in terms of achievement.
- ○ Eliminates 'blind' learning; the students have a clear idea of what they need to do to gain good marks.

Examples of WALT and WILF

Subject	WALT (Objective)	WILF (Outcomes)
English	Writing to persuade – *Develop logical arguments and use supporting evidence, use persuasive writing techniques and rhetorical devices, use appropriate language to gain and sustain reader interest.*	A final piece of writing in the form of an article that persuades the reader not to eat meat, using appropriate and effective persuasive techniques, and a good use of English including spelling, punctuation and grammar.
Maths	Use graphs to interpret and present data – *Collection and interpretation of data, relate summarized data to the question, evaluate and check results, understand correlation, make informed decisions on how best to present the data.*	A planned and researched study detailing how many and what type of pet each class member has. A visual presentation showing the data in an interesting and accurate format using two different types of graph.
Science	Human nutrition – *Understanding the need for a balanced diet, understanding of the principles of digestion, explain the role of enzymes in human digestion, how waste material is egested.*	A detailed, annotated diagram showing the digestion process of humans. A completed worksheet explaining the major food groups and their sources.

LIST 31

Explaining lesson objectives and outcomes

WALT and WILF are simple ways of showing Objectives and Outcomes in every lesson. Often, it is easy to get confused between the two.

○ Lesson objectives are statements that describe the focus and aims of the lesson.

○ Objectives should refer to specific areas for assessment within the curriculum or Key Stages strategies – e.g. geometrical reasoning in Mathematics.

○ Lesson outcomes are what the learners are expected to take away with them during and after the lesson.

○ Outcomes are left more to the teacher's discretion but will be directly linked to the objective – e.g. angles: pupils should be able to distinguish between acute, obtuse, reflex and right angles and estimate the size of an angle in degrees.

○ Both objectives and outcomes are essential parts of good lesson planning and delivery.

○ At the beginning of every lesson, the teacher should explain exactly what the objectives and outcomes are so that no student is in any doubt about:
  1. What they are learning and
  2. What they are expected to achieve.

○ Assessment criteria should clearly match the objectives and outcomes through formative and summative strategies.

○ The teacher should periodically refer back to the objectives and outcomes throughout the lesson to ensure the lesson is on-target and the students are performing to the set criteria.

○ **Remember:** objectives and outcomes are suggested goals, but they do not have to be followed rigidly and can be altered as necessary throughout a lesson or module, thus putting formative assessment to good use.

LIST 32 Linking objectives to outcomes

○ Familiarize yourself with the objectives of the course, subject or module that you are teaching.

○ Ensure you are clear on how the subject will be assessed and how each assessment will link to the objectives and outcomes.

○ Consider your students' skills and abilities in relation to the objectives and how you should approach each section.

○ Define what major outcomes you want your students to achieve in each lesson and throughout the module. Link these to the objectives.

○ Think carefully about knowledge, abilities and resources in terms of yourself as the teacher, and of your students.

○ Create an introductory phase and begin each objective with a brief analysis and explanation that ensures all the students are clear in what is expected of them.

○ After each lesson, go back and check that the outcomes have matched the objectives and that the lesson structure remained on-target.

○ Periodically discuss the lesson objectives and outcomes with your department and with the students to ensure that the required targets are being met successfully.

○ Use formative and summative assessment competently and relevantly to support both objectives and outcomes.

○ Use the four-part lesson-plan structure to support goals and targets within the lesson – Starter – Introduction – Development – Plenary.

○ Use plenary sessions wisely – these are a good opportunity to recap on the objectives and outcomes and to check that ample progress has been made.

LIST 33 Short and long-term strategy planning

All teachers, departments and schools need to work from organized, well-structured strategies to ensure that targets are not only in place, but are being met. Strategies ensure that lessons are properly devised and are goal-orientated, and also ensure the learning route is clearly defined.

○ Strategies are patterns of action, decisions and policies that guide a group towards their goals.
○ They can be short or long-term plans, but need to operate holistically and departmentally.
○ They provide a structure that both students and staff can work from, providing them with an ability to see and understand their targets.
○ Teaching and learning strategies should be concerned with:
  – the subject as a whole (**what**)
  – the teaching methods employed (**how**)
  – the learning environment (**where**)
○ The strategies will provide a framework on which assessment criteria can be modelled.
○ Formative assessment strategies should be strongly linked to subject strategies to ensure that objectives and outcomes have been met.
○ When devising strategies for teaching, learning or assessment, there are a number of key criteria that must be considered.
○ Key Skills will form a foundation structure on which additional strategies can be built.
  For example:
  – problem-solving
  – communication
  – application of number
  – planning
  – teamwork

LIST 34　Using frameworks

As a teacher, you will be expected to use the National Curriculum frameworks in your subject area. It is essential you familiarize yourself with these.

- National Curriculum frameworks provide a list of objectives that state *what* to teach over each academic year.
- The medium-term plan, usually a half-termly document, shows *when* and in what context the material will be taught, e.g. through units of work or specific modules. It will show how much time should be devoted to each area.
- The short-term plan, usually a weekly plan, defines *how* it will be taught and clearly shows how the objectives are to be met.
- Assessment should be continuous throughout the year, with some formal, summative assessment strategy in place to document each individual's achievement.
- All departments should work with each other to ensure there is a whole-school policy on target-setting and achievement strategies.

LIST 35   **Assessment strategies**

As well as using strategies to plan your lessons, you should also formulate strategies that help you when you come to assess the work. The following are crucial questions to consider when thinking about how work will be evaluated.

○ WHAT? – What outcomes/objectives are expected within the lesson/module/year, etc. What is the *reason* for this assessment?
○ HOW? – How will the student be assessed and what key skills will be looked for? How will it be reported or shared? Who is responsible for this assessment taking place?
○ WHERE? – In what environment will the assessment take place – classroom/exam/extracurricular, etc.
○ Will the assessment be summative or formative?
○ Will the results be reported to the student, other staff, parents etc.?
○ Will the assessment have any substantial effect on the learning process as a whole or will it assist the teacher to make informed judgements for teaching and learning?
○ Will this assessment process have any impact on other subjects or will it focus on one specific key area?
○ How will this assessment be differentiated to meet the individual needs of students, for example Gifted and Talented or SEN?
○ How does this assessment process translate to curriculum expectations, whole-school strategies or target levels?
○ What other levels of scope are available to ensure this assessment is valid and correct? For example: department assessment or peer assessment.
○ How will further assessment be monitored and correlated to ensure a visible level of progression?

LIST 36   The bigger picture

Assessment can have both an immediate and long-term effect on the learning process. Grades that seemed important to a student a year ago can lose their importance as time goes by. When explaining assessment processes ensure that:

- The students know what kind of potential impact their final assessment result may have on future achievements – e.g. a piece of coursework completed for GSCE English will contribute to the student's final grade and therefore should be of optimum standard.
- The assessment process is explained in terms of objectives and outcomes so that clear goals and targets are expressed – the students need to know *why* they are being asked to do a certain task.
- Assessment data is collated so that you and the student can monitor progress over time – long-term ipsative assessment helps to track student progress holistically.
- Students are encouraged to reflect on their progress and take an active involvement in their achievement.
- Students understand that their progress and attainment is constantly important, and every single piece of work they do is valued and necessary for future achievements.
- Where assessment is confined to summative forms, take time to emphasize that while good grades are important, continuous achievement is also valuable to the student.

LIST 37 Showing the pupils strategies and goals

A lot of assessment criteria are defined in ways that students may not clearly understand. Teachers should always show their pupils examples of work so they can see the standards they are aiming for. By studying others' completed work, students can develop their reflective skills and take an active part in the assessment process.

Teachers can facilitate this by:

- Showing pupils the learning strategies
- Showing pupils how the assessment criteria have been met in some examples of work from other anonymous students.
- Encouraging students to review examples from anonymous pupils that do *not* meet the assessment criteria. In this way they can reflect on how they might aim higher.
- Encouraging students to assess examples of work from other students in the class to determine if it has met assessment criteria.
- Encouraging students to listen to each other when responding orally and assessing each other's abilities.
- Encouraging self and peer assessment linked to set strategies and mark schemes so that they understand how to tailor their own work to match the assessment strategies.

LIST 38   Involving pupils in their learning

Successful schemes of work identify and show clear learning objectives for a lesson. Lessons are more focused and better paced when teachers share these objectives with their class. In order to involve students in their learning, teachers should:

○ Explain clearly the reasons for the lesson or activity and relate this to the learning objectives.
○ Share the specific assessment criteria with pupils so that they have a clear aim.
○ Help pupils to understand their strengths and weaknesses.
○ Show pupils how to use the assessment criteria to assess their own learning.
○ Give all pupils a chance to interact and contribute to lesson goals.
○ Encourage students to be involved in and contribute to the assessment process.

LIST 39 Useful questions to ask yourself when planning

Designing and planning lessons is not always a straightforward process. To ensure you plan a well-structured and effective lesson, it can be helpful to consider your goal(s) first and then work backwards.

Always ask yourself:

○ What am I aiming to achieve?
○ What are the key areas or knowledge that need to be communicated?
○ How will each outcome link to the specific objective and how can I ensure this happens?
○ What are the specific aims in terms of knowledge, skills, abilities and practice?
○ How are these aims measurable in terms of assessment?
○ What are the long and short-term goals of this lesson?
○ What kind of results am I expecting?
○ How will assessment of this lesson fit in with larger-scale assessment?
○ Does this lesson have any holistic benefits to wider-scale learning and assessment/whole-school issues?
○ How will I use formative or summative assessment within this lesson and what is the purpose behind this assessment?
○ What possible problems might I encounter that will hinder the achievement of each outcome, or the objective as a whole?

Assessment Variations

6

LIST 40 Assessment types

There are many different types of assessment that are suitable for a range of activities and tasks. It is important to match *how* you assess to *what* you are assessing to ensure that you are making the most of the process. Remember, one task can be assessed in a variety of ways. For example: a group activity can lead on to a written task which in turn could be subject to peer evaluation.

The following is by no means a conclusive list, but shows the key crucial types that can be used in any classroom situation.

- Class monitoring – the teacher watches the progress of the class and makes diagnostic decisions regarding behaviour, lesson progress, student ability, etc.
- Class presentations – usually an oral activity where an individual or group presents a report to the class.
- Examinations and tests – can be in a variety of formats. The pupil works individually and is assessed summatively.
- Group assessment – the teacher sets a task for a group of students and assesses the overall performance of the group and each individual within the group.
- Interviewing – teacher–student interaction with focused questions.
- Peer assessment – students judge and comment on others' work in accordance with set guidelines. This can be individually or collaboratively.
- Performance-based assessment – assessment of practical skills in an appropriate environment.
- Portfolios and projects – a selection of work produced by the student that showcases their best work over a period of time.
- Self-assessment – the students assess their own work or performance in accordance with guidelines given by the teacher.

LIST 41 Introducing formal and informal assessment

While very similar to formative and summative assessment, informal and formal assessments are also essential factors in continuous and diagnostic classroom assessment.

Beware: do not get confused by the similarity of the words

Assessment FOR Learning	*Assessment OF Learning*
Formative	Summative
Informal	Formal

Formal assessment

- Like summative assessment
- Standardized
- Assesses individual knowledge and learning
- Records progress and ability
- Requires individual thinking
- Usually set to specific timescales
- Rigid form

Informal assessment

- Like formative assessment
- Standardized and non-standardized
- Guided instruction
- Used periodically
- Monitors skills and level of learning
- Can be timed or ongoing
- Usually more relaxed

Formal and informal ideas

Formal Assessment

○ Written tests/exams – assess understanding, reading and writing ability and level of response. These can be school, department or state-set tests and the results can be used as is appropriate to the importance of the exam.

○ Skills tests – examine understanding and ability in specific skills and strategies taught over a set period. These can be written (e.g. humanities and literature), oral (e.g. English skills, MFL) or practical (e.g. cookery, Arts, PE) depending on the subject.

○ Spelling/numeracy tests – identify pupils' level of learning and understanding.

○ Mock exam practice – gives pupils valuable exam experience and requires high performance under specific guidelines. Gives pupils a realistic idea of what to expect in an exam.

Informal Assessment

○ Group or individual projects.

○ Oral presentations or performances.

○ Reading assessments (close reading, book reports, etc.).

○ Essays, homework, journals, reading records – as part of the usual teaching quota.

○ Observation of class or individual to deduce how the student is performing.

○ Class or individual feedback regarding the lesson objective/outcome, or the specific set task.

○ Differentiated tasks to actively meet the needs of the individual.

LIST 43   Grades v assessment

Assessment and grades are not the same thing, but they do overlap.
The following table serves well to highlight the differences between
the two.

Assessment	Grades
Formative	Summative
Informal	Formal
Continuous/ongoing	Decisive/final
Specific	Holistic
Usually non-judgemental	Evaluative
Variety of forms	Mainly test or exam-based
Monitors how the student performs on a long-term scale	Monitors how the student performed on that day

Diagnostic assessment

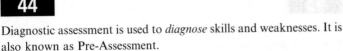

Diagnostic assessment is used to *diagnose* skills and weaknesses. It is also known as Pre-Assessment.

It is generally used as an initial form of assessment, but is also strongly linked with continuous formative strategies.

This form of assessment is especially useful for assessing new students, students returning to school after time away or for streaming pupils according to ability.

Diagnostic assessment evaluates:

○ What level of skills and knowledge the student has already achieved.
○ What skills and knowledge the students can bring with them into the course.
○ Any gaps or weaknesses that are apparent in the student's knowledge compared to others of a similar age and ability.
○ Any potential factors that may have an impact on how the student learns: e.g. SEN, first language other than English, behavioural issues.
○ Any additional requirements the student may have in terms of differentiating learning and meeting learning needs.

Diagnostic assessment takes many forms:

○ Interviewing the student.
○ Discussion with parents/carers/other educational professionals who have close links to the student.
○ Summative assessment of any previous work or test results.
○ Subject-specific skills tests or concept tests.
○ Close monitoring and tracking of pupil progression.

In order for assessment to work effectively, it must be a continuous process. There is little point awarding grades, scores and praise if they don't mean anything to the student.

As well as being an effective monitoring tool, continuous assessment helps the student to feel valued and to feel that learning and achievement has a purpose.

Continuous assessment is a form of formative and ipsative assessment – it records current progress in relation to past achievements, and helps to determine how best to continue.

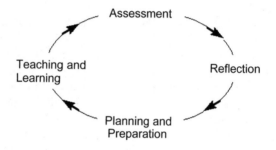

- ○ Assessment – the systematic observation of the students and collection of evidence to document how they are learning and improving in relation to what they have been taught.
- ○ Reflection – the examination of the students' work to determine strengths and weaknesses and possible needs.
- ○ Planning and Preparation – organizing teaching methods to address students' strengths and weaknesses.
- ○ Teaching and Learning – the delivery of lessons and instructional material by the teacher to the student.

Continuous assessment:

- ○ Covers all areas of assessment – academic, behavioural, social and vocational.
- ○ Records pupil progress and allows them to see improvements over time.

- Acts as an essential diagnostic tool for assessing pupil progress and target setting.
- Allows monitoring of teaching effectiveness and impact on learning.
- Allows a teacher to adjust his/her pedagogical strategies to ensure all students are being provided for.
- Assists in the implementation of differentiation strategies.
- Encourages teacher–pupil interaction
- Puts learning in the 'bigger picture'.
- Evaluates the student as a whole rather than merely concentrating on one area.
- Encourages motivation and drive to succeed.
- Puts the emphasis on skills and abilities rather than grades and scores.
- Helps students to visualize their goals and implement strategies to achieve them.
- Helps to ensure that assessment is a whole-school issue and encourages departments to work together.

Self-assessment

Not all assessment has to be done by teachers or assessment boards. Self-assessment is also an essential part of pupil progress.

○ Self-assessment helps to promote ownership of learning and encourages the student to take responsibility for his or her own education.

○ It encourages the student to be aware of his or her own learning process and subsequently the areas where development and improvement are needed.

○ It promotes self-awareness and involvement in the education system.

○ It eliminates the danger of damage to self-esteem; skills and weaknesses can be identified on a personal level.

○ It promotes an active interest in learning and development and encourages the desire to engage in the learning process; it can make learning seem fun.

○ When implemented within a group, students can learn from their peers and gauge how others are doing while learning from, and helping, each other through interpersonal learning.

Making self-assessment work

Self-assessment is a powerful part of assessment for learning (formative assessment). It encourages pupils to engage in their learning, become more interested in how they learn and can help them to evaluate their own skills and weaknesses. In turn, this helps them to grow and improve.

Self-assessment helps pupils to:

○ Reflect on and evaluate their progress and achievement.
○ Identify and approach problem areas without risk to their self-esteem.
○ Accept responsibility for their own learning while receiving the support to achieve high goals.
○ See assessment in a positive light – rather than teachers passing judgement on them, they are in control of their progress.

To ensure self-assessment is truly useful, teachers must:

○ provide the criteria to self-assess against
○ ensure the assessment is firm but fair – strengths *and* weaknesses must be identified in order to improve
○ pupils must have a good understanding of how and what they are assessing
○ any evaluations must be supported with evidence
○ goals and targets should be clear – the student must know what they want to get out of it

Examples of self-assessment

Self-assessment is not solely confined to the grading or self-analysis of work, it is also present in other forms such as:

○ Weekly student planners/diaries
○ Questionnaires
○ Portfolios
○ Marking of own work with reference to specific criteria or targets
○ Self-assessment sheets where the pupils comment on their own work/performance
○ Oral feedback in class
○ Group/individual discussion
○ Personal statements for report cards or records of achievement
○ Preparation and planning towards a final piece of work
○ Analysis of assessment criteria and ability to relate this to their own work

LIST 49 Learning from mistakes

Challenges can be stepping stones or stumbling blocks, it's just a matter of how you view them. Unknown

Much of experience is gained through making mistakes. Every human, student and teacher, will make mistakes. When mistakes are made, often the individual will have feelings of failure, which can lead to low self-esteem and loss of confidence.

Learning from mistakes is merely another form of self-assessment; it shows you can recognize your faults and turn negative experiences into positive ones in the future.

To help both you and your students learn from mistakes:

○ Attempt to identify any potential problems before you start – this does not mean anticipating the worst, merely preparing for every eventuality.
○ Admit you have made a mistake and move on from it – dwelling on failure will only damage your self-esteem.
○ Give yourself or the student the permission to make mistakes – no one is perfect and no one can get everything right all the time.
○ See mistakes as a challenge or progress – making a mistake means you need to try a new approach.
○ Analyse the mistake – try to figure out where you went wrong and how you might put it right.
○ Talk about your mistakes – a problem shared is a problem halved and other people may be able to offer ideas you hadn't thought of.
○ Focus on the positive – think about what went right as opposed to what went wrong. Praise yourself or your students on their achievements no matter how small.
○ Do not 'beat yourself up' over a mistake – even mistakes that seem catastrophic can be fixable.
○ Keep your sense of humour – it is far better to laugh about a mistake and move on than to feel miserable and dwell on it.
○ **Remember:** identifying and learning from a mistake is an important area of self-assessment.

Peer assessment

Peer assessment encourages teamwork and communication between all learners. It allows students to become actively involved in the learning process and to engage with their peers.

Peer assessment is similar to self-assessment, but it also:

○ Encourages students to take responsibility for, and take an active part in, their own learning.
○ Gives a sense of ownership of the assessment process.
○ Improves motivation and development.
○ Shows how assessment has a positive contribution to learning.
○ Encourages reflection and personal analysis as part of the learning process.
○ Prepares students for peer assessment and examination in later life.
○ Encourages communication and respect for others.
○ Assists the ability to make sensitive and thoughtful judgements about others.
○ Assists the self-assessment process.
○ Helps to empower students by giving them control of their own learning and progression.
○ Allows the teacher to shift the focus from assessing the task to assessing the student – by allowing students to assess themselves and each other, the teacher can in turn assess the social and life skills of the students in how they engage or interact with others.

L I S T 51 Ground rules for peer assessment

Peer assessment can sometimes be a tricky form to use effectively. It is essential you explain to the students what you expect them to do and what they will get out of the process. Always ensure you set ground rules before asking students to assess their peers.

- Students should always identify strengths before weaknesses.
- Ensure the focus stays on improvement and positive evaluation rather than criticism.
- Give individuals a chance to comment on their own skills and weaknesses before allowing others to contribute.
- Feedback should be relevant, constructive and fair.
- Comments must be supported with evidence – do not allow generalized statements.
- Ensure the feedback is clear and informative and can be easily understood.
- Disallow any feedback that is derogatory, offensive or negative without good cause.
- **Remember:** while the students assess themselves or each other, you must also be continuously assessing *them*.
- **Do not** use peer or self-assessment to take the place of teacher assessment.

Dangers of peer assessment

Before you consider using peer assessment in the classroom, make sure you are aware of the potential pitfalls.

- Some students may lack the ability to make informed judgements or evaluations.
- Discrimination and friendship issues may affect how pupils judge each other.
- Pupils may not take the exercise seriously enough to ensure the assessment is correct and valid.
- Without accurate teacher intervention, students may purposely or accidentally misinform each other.
- Students may not understand the marking criteria well enough to make accurate analysis.
- Pupils may be over-zealous or miss important points, making the assessment less valid.

Examples of peer assessment

As well as the obvious example of students swapping their books to mark in class, there are also other interesting and effective ways of using peer assessment.

- Class review of individual or group performance (speaking, listening, drama, written work, etc.).
- Formal group discussions based on a task done in class.
- Marking of others' work in relation to specific criteria – e.g. swapping books to mark a test in class.
- Examining and grading examples of past work – e.g. assessing good and bad examples of work and being able to state why they are good or bad.
- Formal or informal discussions and feedback.
- Group work to encourage teamwork and communication – e.g. a class 'challenge' or role-play session.
- Group or pair projects that necessitate good communication and evaluation of each other's work.

LIST 54

Performance-based assessment

Rather than confine assessment to written or oral tasks, it is also useful to use performance-based assessment to encourage students to think about the different ways of approaching a task.

- Performance-based assessment is sometimes known as alternative assessment.
- Students are required to perform a task rather than sit a test or exam.
- Examples of performance-based assessment include:
  - explaining a historical event
  - solving a mathematical problem or scientific experiment
  - conversing in a foreign language
  - conducting research on a specific topic or area
- *Extended tasks* require sustained attention to one set work area. These can include drafting, reviewing and revising a piece of writing; conducting and explaining a scientific experiment; researching, sketching and painting a set piece of art work.
- *Open-ended or extended response exercises* are questions or prompts that require students to explore a topic in writing. This could be a critical essay, observations from a science experiment or explaining a religious belief or historical movement.
- *Portfolios* are selected collections of pupils' performance-based work. They usually include the students' best work, and may include works in progress that show how the student has developed over time. Portfolios often include a pupil self-evaluation of the work included.
- Performance-based assessment assesses how the student has done a practical task, but is still graded in accordance with set levels and standards.
- Performance-based assessment is widely used in vocational and 'hands-on' subjects such as Physical Education, Cookery or Design Technology, but can be used in all subjects.
- It allows teachers to see a type of 'active' learning in the classroom, and see how academic and vocational performances differ with varying stimulus.
- Some teachers find that using a checklist to assist performance-based assessment gives them a clearer idea of what skills they are looking for in an active learning environment – e.g.

- does the student show awareness of what is expected of him/her?
- does the student show awareness and understanding of the objectives of the task?
- has the student recognized the outcomes of the task and is he/she working accordingly?
- has the student planned his/her response to the task appropriately?
- can the student communicate his/her plans for the task?

Group assessment

Teaching and learning are very much based on communication. To encourage effective communication between your students, you may wish to consider the use of group assessment.

○ Group assessment can be done by:
  a) assessing each individual's strengths and weaknesses and combining the 'scores', or
  b) assessing the entire group as a whole on its strengths and weaknesses to ascertain a final grade
○ Ensure all students are clear that they will be assessed as a group, and as such must work together to attain a good grade.

Consider:

○ The level of communication between each individual within the group.
○ The level of understanding towards the task and how it has been interpreted.
○ Is there evidence to show consideration for the audience?
○ Is there evidence to show the group has an understanding of how each individual should interact with the others and with the audience?
○ How the group performs as a unit – are there signs of leadership, reluctance, domination or delegation?
○ Is there evidence that the speakers are listening to each other as well as performing individually?
○ Does the group use correct vocabulary and terminology?
○ Does the group expand upon points made by individuals, or is each member merely putting forward his/her own point of view?
○ Does the group show flair and originality in their work or presentation?
○ Is there evidence to show that the group understands their priorities?
○ Is there evidence to show that the members of the group are supporting each other?

LIST 56 Portfolios

Portfolios are an excellent way of showing an assessor the wide range of different skills a student has mastered over time.

○ Portfolios are often used in conjunction with performance-based assessment, and often help to make up a large section of final grades in Key Stage 4 and 5 assessments.
○ They can be an integral part of self-assessment and learning development.
○ Portfolios usually show: the student's best work, progression of how they have come to complete the final piece and self-reflection or evaluation.
○ Although there are many uses and reasons for portfolios, two major categories are Assessment and Instruction.
○ They are readily adaptable to any age, ability or motivational level.
○ They can be integrated into the curriculum and show records of student progress.
○ A successful portfolio helps to support:
  – goal/target setting
  – self-evaluation and positive personal criticism
  – a heightened awareness of and responsibility for individual learning
  – close personal examination of achievement
  – the identification of strengths and weaknesses over a set time period
  – encouragement of concise planning and the motivation to complete a task
  – the desire to show off students' best assets and 'sell' themselves through their achievements
  – self-esteem and taking pride in work

English

- autobiographies
- poetry compilations
- essay writing
- creative writing skills
- critical analysis of text
- newspaper/advertisement production

Mathematics

- problem-solving
- data analysis
- statistical studies
- presenting problems

Science

- experiments and analysis
- in-depth scientific studies
- research skills
- topic-specific areas of study

Modern Foreign Languages

- example pieces of text written in an MFL
- translation skills
- design of advertisements/articles in an MFL
- use or design of maps/pamphlets in an MFL

Art & Design and Technology

- examples of styles, skills, colour awareness, form, texture, etc.
- showing the use of varying mediums
- understanding of historical art movements
- sketching examples
- showing working progression towards a final piece
- examples of work
- practical skills
- presentation ability and communication through artistic medium

Physical Education, Dance & Drama

○ understanding/awareness of physical fitness/health and safety
○ choreography skills
○ use of shape, form, strength, etc.
○ techniques, scripts, team structures, etc.

Student-designed assessment

Not all assessment needs to be performed by a teacher. In some subjects it can be enlightening to let the students themselves decide how a task should be assessed and let them administer self or peer assessment [Note: this kind of assessment is usually more suited to creative subjects], e.g.

Drama and Dance: students perform a piece for the rest of the group and their peers provide critical feedback.

English: group work and oral work can be assessed by the students' peers based on performance or delivery.

Mathematics: pupils work individually on an exercise and are given the answers when it is complete to mark their own work.

○ Assessment can be through oral feedback or discussion, or by allowing the students to offer grades based on the work they have seen.

○ Self-assessment and reflection will also be integral components of this form of assessment.

Allowing the students to decide how assessment should take place also assists the teacher in assessing their understanding of the assessment – a cyclical assessment process.

LIST 59 Mock exams

Mock exams are an important assessment tool. They can provide opportunities for staff and students to assess current skills and determine targets for improvement. In order for mocks to be efficient, it is essential they be treated with as much seriousness as a 'real' exam.

Remember: the objective is to give students an opportunity to experience as close to real exam conditions as possible, and assess them on their performance at that time.

Benefits

- practice in answering exam-based questions
- experience of exam conditions and organizing time management
- practice of exam techniques
- experience of sustained academic testing
- help staff determine students' strengths and weaknesses
- indicative of pupil progress and ability
- help to determine what levels students should be entered at in real exams
- encourage revision methods and practice
- the scores do not count towards final marks – students have a chance to improve before the final exam
- less stressful method of formative assessment
- gives teachers a chance to improve their exam marking skills.

Drawbacks

- disrupt valuable teaching and learning time
- they can mean extra and unnecessary work for staff and students
- they are not appropriate for all courses
- most students already have plenty of exam practice
- changes to the curriculum can make past exam papers irrelevant
- students do not always take them seriously, making the results flawed
- extra time needs to be spent on organizing mocks
- not all schools can spare the space needed to hold mocks
- extra work for teachers through planning, preparation and marking.

Student Variations

 Age

As students move through the varying stages of their education, the assessment criteria through which they are monitored will change dramatically.

For any assessor, it is essential that:

- ❍ The level of assessment be appropriate to the level of the material being taught and learned.
- ❍ Continuous assessment across the key stages be an integral part of teaching and learning for every individual.
- ❍ Opportunities be provided for students who are working above or below recommended National Curriculum levels in accordance with the Inclusion strategy.
- ❍ The level of assessment will invariably change according to pupil age groups, but the quality and tone of assessment should remain positive and appraising regardless of age or achievement.
- ❍ In every age group, the assessment process should be fully explained to the students so that they are clear about the targets they are aiming for.

LIST 61 Gender

This is a general guide designed to make you aware of the most common learning issues regarding gender. It does not necessarily apply to all students of that gender.

❍ Boys tend to be weaker in:
  - language acquisition, reading and writing tasks
  - concentrating and motivating themselves
  - understanding the 'bigger picture'
  - completing a task
  - communication skills

❍ Girls tend to be weaker in:
  - visual and spatial problems
  - logical or mathematical formulae

❍ Boys tend to be stronger in:
  - three-dimensional or spatial problems
  - visual, aural and kinaesthetic learning
  - vocational, 'hands-on' skills
  - competitive tests, especially physical skills

❍ Girls tend to be stronger in:
  - understanding the 'bigger picture'
  - language acquisition, reading and writing ability
  - imagination and creative tasks
  - concentration and motivation
  - sharing and cooperating with others
  - communication skills

English as an Additional Language (EAL) students

○ Many students who may originate from overseas, or are born into a non-English-speaking culture, may speak, understand or be literate in other languages. In many instances English is not their first language, but in the majority of UK schools this is the language they will be taught in.

○ The skills and abilities of these students may vary due to a number of different factors such as age, gender and previous schooling. All students in the UK education system have a right to a broad and varied curriculum, whether or not English is their first language.

○ Schools can apply for extra support in order to help them cope with the demands of EAL students. Interpreters, bilingual staff and appropriate bilingual resources all help to integrate the student into the education system in accordance with government inclusion policies.

○ For any new EAL student accepted into the school, initial assessment is essential to determine what skills the pupil already has, and what opportunities need to be made available to reduce any potential learning barriers for the student.

○ In an initial interview, the school should gain access to the student's ethnicity, first language, any previous educational achievements and experience. This will also help to assess the student's level of fluency in English.

○ Initial assessment will also help to eliminate any self-esteem issues or worries that an EAL student may have at entering an English-speaking school for the first time. It is important to ensure every student feels included in the educational system.

○ It is important that EAL students are not automatically placed in lower streams or ability groups. Speaking an additional language should not be regarded as an obstacle to learning, and previous academic achievements must be recognized within the classroom.

○ In order to remove initial barriers, it is essential that EAL students are:
  – given opportunities to use their first language skills
  – given appropriate resources which use effective visual representation and explanation techniques where necessary
  – given differentiated opportunities within the classroom
  – provided with the option of differentiated assessment criteria, that handle their use of English sensitively and appropriately.

LIST 63 Special Educational Needs students

○ A child is considered to have Special Educational Needs if he or she has a learning difficulty that requires special educational provision to be made for them.

○ Although many children may have learning difficulties, a child will be added to a school's SEN register if the difficulty is seen to be significantly greater than that of the majority of other students of the same age.

○ The SEN register should be available to all members of staff to ensure they are all aware of each student's needs.

○ As with all students, SEN students need to have their performance reviewed regularly and their progress reported.

○ SENs should be taken into account when making any assessment of a pupil.

○ Particularly consider literacy and numeracy difficulties when making any type of assessment.

○ SENs also cover emotional and behavioural needs and it is imperative that any assessment be empathetic to the child.

○ When appropriate, Individual Learning Plans will assist with assessment to track progress and involve the student in their targets.

○ A SEN does not necessarily mean the student will have a lower ability, and it is essential to stretch their skills as much as those of any other student.

○ For some SEN students, normal curriculum levels may not be appropriate.

○ Performance Criteria Scales (P Scales) are recommended by the DfES and can be used with SEN students between the ages of 5 and 16 working under usually expected curriculum levels.

○ P Scales are used to assess English and Mathematics. They can be used to:
    – show that SEN students are making progress although this progress may not be fully obvious in terms of the NC
    – help provide meaningful targets for SEN students in a whole-school setting.
    – help to explain the achievements of SEN students more clearly, especially when reporting to parents, or other professionals in the education field.

Gifted and Talented students

○ Gifted and Talented students are identified through their aptitude, talents and skills in a variety of subjects, although they may show outstanding achievement in only two or three subjects.

○ A student may also be classed as G&T if they show exceptional achievement across the curriculum.

○ Most G&T students will be working in the top 5–10 per cent of any school regardless of the overall ability of other students.

○ All G&T students should be assessed regularly and their performance should be reported.

○ It is essential that G&T students be kept challenged and their abilities exercised across the school.

○ Additional curriculum levels may be appropriate for these students in conjunction with the provision of extra activities.

○ Many G&T students may require accelerated learning and additional support to ensure they are reaching their full potential.

○ Day to day formative assessment and peer assessment is particularly useful, as G&T students benefit from a wide range of encouragement and target setting.

○ Rigorous formative assessment can ensure that G&T students are consistently improving, and can help build further targets for higher-level learning.

○ Modelling through assessment encourages ownership of learning and a greater level of student involvement. This in turn will accelerate the student's understanding and drive to succeed.

○ All methods of assessment will ensure that any potential hurdles are identified and targets are put in place to remove them.

○ Teachers who teach higher-level learning should be aware of how they can encourage and improve teaching and learning within the classroom through differentiation and accelerated learning groups.

LIST 65 Underachievement

○ A student may be considered to be underachieving if he/she is not working at the expected National Curriculum levels compared to other students of similar age and ability.

○ Although many underachievers may have a SEN, which may affect their attainment, this is not always the case.

○ Underachievement is more often noted in young males, but it is also apparent in many young females.

○ There are many factors that contribute to underachievement, but it has been noted that many students who are poor academically will also exhibit poor behaviour issues.

○ Initial assessment should determine if this underachievement is:
  – linked to any particular change in Key Stage or if it has always been apparent.
  – noticeable in all subjects or just a select few
  – due to poor behaviour or attitude
  – linked to any particular subject, class, teacher or group
  – due to real difficulties on the student's part, or if the student has not been supported or challenged enough
  – linked to any possible SEN or medical problem
  – an individual problem or a class issue that may suggest possible teaching problems

○ Continuous assessment of underachievement should provide encouragement and target-setting to assist the pupils, not judge them.

○ Individual Learning Plans or Individual Behaviour Plans may be appropriate for underachievers to monitor their progress formally.

○ Underachievement must be tackled holistically and the whole school should be involved in raising achievement.

○ An underachiever may need additional support within the classroom, which should be recognized in any assessment process.

LIST 66 Differentiation

○ Differentiation involves teaching the same curriculum to students of all ranges and abilities by successfully using teaching strategies and resources to meet the varied needs of each individual.

○ Differentiation and inclusion go hand in hand in the National Curriculum and serve to ensure all students are being given the standard of education that they deserve.

○ When planning, teachers should provide opportunities for all students to achieve, while maintaining high standards.

○ Differentiation provides students with a system of equality, ensuring that each individual is recognized on his/her own merits and given the chance to succeed.

○ Differentiation puts the emphasis on what is learnt rather than what is taught, providing an effective and universal curriculum.

○ To ensure differentiation is effective, teachers must consider:
  – the needs of each student
  – the skills and abilities of each student
  – the objectives and outcomes and how these might change between individuals or groups
  – the level of resources and assistance available
  – how achievement will be monitored and assessed

○ Teachers must not make assumptions when differentiating lessons, nor when considering the ability of the child; they must explore any differences and tailor their teaching effectively.

○ Involve other teachers and departments when planning for differentiation – consider whole-school approaches and utilize tried and tested methods that work.

○ Consider assessment methods that complement differentiation rather than focus on it, e.g. when asking dyslexic students to write a creative story, allowing them to use ICT to produce their final paper will take the focus off their spelling skills and put it more on their writing ability.

Remember: differentiation should be considered in classes of all ages and abilities to encourage a high standard of learning. This includes:
  – Gifted and Talented students
  – Students with Special Educational Needs or disabilities
  – students with behavioural issues

- students from varying social and cultural backgrounds
- gender differences
- students from varying ethnic groups (including asylum seekers, travellers, etc.)
- students with varying linguistic backgrounds (ESOL, etc.)

Home-schooled students

○ Although UK law states that all children are required to have some form of formal education from the age of 5 to 16, they are not required to receive this education at school.

○ Home schooling is considered a perfectly acceptable method of educating your child, providing that it follows a format that:
  – prepares children for life in a modern, civilized society
  – ensures that the child is achieving to his/her full potential

○ Children schooled at home do not have to follow the National Curriculum, and are not required to meet any government achievement standards.

○ Children who have been home-schooled and are entering school-based education are unlikely to have been formally assessed at any NC level.

○ Initial, diagnostic assessment for a home-schooled child beginning his or her education at school should include assessment of some examples of the pupil's work to assess his/her skills and abilities.

○ The child may be formally assessed in accordance with appropriate Key Stage tests to realize their current skill level.

○ It is essential that work be done with the students to ensure they are integrated into the school system quickly and without fuss.

○ Treat home-schooled students as you would any new student to the school.

○ **Remember:** home schooling can be very different to school-based education. Much of what happens in a school is normal to most children but may be confusing or difficult for a child unused to this type of education.

Marking, Monitoring and Recording

8

LIST 68 Giving good feedback

Giving feedback, either oral or written, is an essential element in assessment for learning. Teachers should be clear, fair and concise when giving feedback so as not to damage the pupil's self-esteem.

Pupils also benefit from formal feedback in group, or plenary sessions. If this is used well it allows the pupils to see for themselves what they need to do to improve rather than relying on the teacher to tell them.

○ Feedback is most effective when it focuses on the task, is given regularly and while still relevant.
○ Good feedback should provoke the desire to expand and improve current skills to ensure that learning is continuous.
○ Feedback is most effective when it shows students they are progressing on the right track and allows them to correct or improve their own work.
○ Feedback should be a stepping-stone for pupil improvement. The pupils should be given suggestions for improvement, not spoon-fed right and wrong answers, so that they can learn and think for themselves.
○ It is more beneficial to offer feedback on a number of attempts rather than one sole area or piece of work.
○ If pupils continue to make the same errors after multiple explanations, then an alternative method of feedback should be considered.
○ Oral feedback is more effective than written and more likely to engage the pupils and stimulate them to improve.
○ Feedback should encourage students to ask for help and to take an active approach to their learning.

L I S T 69 Making comments relevant

There is no doubt that marking books takes up a lot of teachers' time. It can be easy to let your marking standards fall by slipping into the habit of leaving only very short, or generalized comments.

To avoid comments being meaningless and unhelpful, you must always ensure that any comments you give are goal-orientated and relevant.

Your objective in any marking task is to:

a) alert the student to their mistakes and
b) offer realistic and positive suggestions for improvement

Always avoid simply giving out the answer – spoon-feeding will not encourage a student to learn; you will simply be wasting your time and theirs.

- Be very clear on the objectives and outcomes of the task and what you are assessing.
- Consistently praise good work.
- If the student has made a mistake, explain why and how they might improve next time.
  'Your diagrams show you have not used a ruler. Make sure you use one next time and you will gain a better mark.'
- Link comments to standards or assessment criteria, do not make generalized statements:
  'You have shown a good understanding of the ways meaning and information are conveyed.'
  'You have made sensible estimates of a range of measures.'
- Inform the student how they might attain a higher grade next time:
  'At the moment you are working at level 4. To gain a level 5 you could ...'
- Encourage reflective learning and self-evaluation:
  'Always make sure you check your work before you hand it in.'
  'I believe that if you do more work on ... you will get a better mark next time.'
- Refer back to previous work to show how the student has improved:
  'Your use of punctuation has noticeably improved since your last assignment.'

L I S T 70 Successful marking

Just as important as making relevant comments is ensuring your marking is successful. 'Blind' marking, which does not help the student improve, is simply a waste of time for everyone. Regardless of the task, whether it is an end of unit essay or a simple Mathematics quiz, always consider the following when marking pupils' work.

○ Marking should be fair, encouraging and proactive.
○ While marking, always consider the What, How and Where of assessment strategies.
○ Remember even basic-level assessment can be linked to National Curriculum attainment targets.
○ Ensure your comments are concise, legible and informative.
○ Use recognized marking formats agreed by your department or school.
○ Are you and your students clear about what you are looking for?
○ Is it your sole responsibility for marking or can it be done as a whole department or as a class exercise (peer assessment)?
○ Be wary of using too much red pen, keep alterations or comments simple and don't cover the whole work.
○ Red is a negative colour – try to mark in blue or green to encourage positive self-esteem.
○ Crosses are a negative symbol – where possible use a slash (/) rather than a cross (X) when marking a wrong answer.
○ Never make negative comments on students' work, even if their work is bad or wrong.
○ Review the quality of work in terms of previous achievements as well as a singular piece.
○ Be aware of how you are marking: does the work need a further comment or can it be marked with a score?
○ Is a 'well done' or 'keep it up' just as helpful as a detailed comment?
○ Is it necessary to provide a follow-up of the work in class, for example, if a large proportion of students has made the same mistakes?
○ Keep marking up to date at all times!

Appropriateness to form

Assessment is only going to be useful if you use it to mean something. There is little point collecting grades and marks if they merely sit in a filing cabinet and are stored away.

Remember: Effective assessment encourages improvement and promotes further learning.

Before you begin any evaluation process, always consider the following points:

○ Always ensure you know what outcomes you are looking for in any assessment.
○ Ensure the method of assessment matches the task.
○ Consider how the assessment will take place and be delivered: will it be oral praise, written comments or a score/grade?
○ Consider the age group, Key Stage and ability of the student. Encourage students to aim high but don't knock them down if they fail to achieve high standards.
○ Ask yourself why this assessment is important and what is its purpose?
○ Who will see these results? Will they be shared with parents or other teachers, or are they just for you and your students?
○ How detailed does your assessment need to be on this particular task?
○ Consider the impact your assessment will have on self-esteem.
○ Consider how the results (if any) will be used at a later date as well as the present time.

The three-rule marking strategy

Getting the balance right when leaving comments on work can be awkward. There is always the danger of writing too much or too little, or perhaps unintentionally upsetting students by being too harsh.

The objective of marking is to encourage improvement and recognize achievement.

Remember: having someone else point out your mistakes is never a pleasant process for anyone. Even if a student has done quite poorly in the task, never be overly critical or derisive.

You may find it helpful to remember this strategy as '*A Star, A Rainbow and A Wish*'.

1. *A Star:* Always show praise or encouragement regardless of the overall standard of work produced. Negative comments will not help the student strive to achieve.
2. *A Rainbow:* Highlight key areas of both good and bad work – if the student has made mistakes, point these out, but ensure this is done sensitively. Try to avoid the word 'but'. There is no point building a student up just to push them down again.
3. *A Wish:* Offer suggestions on how to improve or put mistakes right. Again, keep these positive and informative.

Examples of the three-rule marking strategy

'This is a very well presented and thoughtful piece of writing. I am very impressed by your creative writing skills, although I feel you need to do more work on your spelling and punctuation. I will issue you with your own spelling diary to help you improve.'

'You have obviously tried very hard with this task and you have got many answers correct. You have lost some marks because you did not show your working out – always remember to show how you have reached your answer.'

'This is a very well done piece of homework. You have obviously listened well in class and your experiment report is very detailed. You have often confused millilitres with litres, always check through your work before you hand it in.'

Marking tips

Every subject will have its own specific key tips for successful marking, but as a general rule:

- Always work from a rigid, standardized marking scheme – this may be a departmental scheme or a national standards scheme.
- Be very clear about what you are looking for and what you need to mark.
- Look for areas to praise rather than faults to mark wrong.
- Mark in ink a different colour to the script.
- If you are in any doubt, make notations in pencil and refer back to marking schemes to gain an accurate total.
- Write the marks on the script at the point they were earned – this makes adding up the total a lot easier.
- Always indicate which section you have marked, at least with a tick.
- Use a rigid structure for showing mistakes or errors: e.g. circle spelling mistakes, underline errors.
- Record all the marks for the questions answered clearly either on the front page of the exam script or on a candidate record form.
- Annotate the script with brief but relevant comments where necessary.
- Make note of any omitted sections if necessary.
- Check and double-check the totals to ensure you have not missed any sections.

Marking exam papers

Although it is highly unlikely that you will ever be asked to mark any of your students' final exams, you may be expected to mark any mock exams that take place within your school. Always make sure you take any exam marking, real or mock, very seriously.

○ Acquire accurate and up-to-date copies of level descriptors, marking schemes and sample materials.
○ Take the time to familiarize yourself with these marking schemes.
○ Be clear on the assessment objectives of the paper(s)/tasks
○ Only assess material according to the relevant assessment objectives.
○ Be positive when marking – look for achievements rather than weaknesses.
○ Comments should focus on the assessment objectives – use clear annotations that demonstrate how the assessment objectives have been met.
○ Use the full range of available marks, particularly when marking higher-level papers.
○ Show evidence that you have read every page by marking each assessed page with a tick.
○ Work through the paper carefully and systematically – double-check the points you award/comments you make.
○ Liaise with your department and discuss effective ways to mark.
○ Use contact time with your department to discuss marking practices and learn from each other.
○ Always mark in ink.

Monitoring and tracking

Monitoring and tracking pupils can be both a formal and informal process. You may decide to monitor a child due to having some specific concerns, or perhaps you simply want to check how they have progressed in certain areas. Whatever the reason, taking an active interest in your pupils will help you spot any potential problems or areas for improvement early on.

- ○ Monitoring and tracking are variations of formative assessment and can be linked to academic achievement, behaviour or even just self-esteem and well-being.
- ○ All teachers should constantly and consistently monitor their students' progress both academically and personally as part of their essential teaching skills.
- ○ Monitoring can be a formal process and recorded, or it can be as simple as a teacher asking students how they feel about a subject or class.
- ○ Successful monitoring involves collaborative assessment between the student, teachers and the whole school or department.
- ○ Monitoring and tracking should be part of a diagnostic process and should investigate the development of learning in relation to what has been taught.

Pupil progress

Some students may benefit from teacher tracking to ensure that any problem areas can be monitored and addressed effectively.

Monitoring and tracking are useful for all students, not just those with difficulties, and it can be just as revealing to track a high-achiever as a lower one.

○ Draw up a time frame in which formal assessment should take place, e.g. half-termly, every two weeks, at the end of each module.

○ Identify the key areas where the student will be monitored and assessed. These can be on a wide variety of areas such as: writing, reading, speaking, homework, behaviour or attendance.

○ Keep accurate and concise records that detail pupil achievement in these key areas. Always keep any paperwork up to date.

○ Always keep a copy of these records either electronically or in hard format, and where possible keep these records at the school. Although most teachers take work home to mark, it is not always possible to guarantee that things do not get lost in transit.

○ If assessment is made in grade/level format, use a database or chart to keep levels of achievement in an easy to review format. Lots of notes and numbers will not mean much to you or the student unless they correspond to key areas.

○ Stick to a unified marking system: don't switch from lettered grades to numbered levels halfway through. Similarly, always update records at regular intervals.

○ If you intend to monitor a student over a set time scale, ensure you stick to this. Don't stop monitoring just because you see improvement, make sure it is an ongoing process.

○ Using visual methods such as bar charts or line graphs can easily highlight levels of achievement or problem areas. When monitoring behaviour, consider using a 'smiley' chart or gold stars to measure achievement.

○ Always share your monitoring data with the student, your department and the whole school. Results are meaningless unless they exist to serve a purpose.

L I S T 78   **Classroom monitoring skills**

Monitoring in the classroom is the one definite way of making sure your teaching is as effective as you want it to be. It is no good delivering a fantastic lesson if you have lost all your students in the first five minutes.

○ Check all students understand the material being taught and what is expected of them throughout the lesson.

○ Circulate around the classroom and engage in one-to-one questioning regarding their work.

○ Assign relevant homework and ensure it is collected, marked and returned as necessary, and keep accurate and up-to-date records on each individual's achievement.

○ Frequently review student performance and use this data proactively to plan successful lessons or learning resources.

○ Engage with the students to confirm their level of understanding regarding the learning material and the skills they have gained.

○ Where appropriate, assign and assess tests and exams, keeping a good record of pupil scores.

○ Take an active interest in the pupil both inside and outside the classroom and promote a positive and happy relationship.

○ Always consider outside influences or factors that may affect pupil progress, and ensure differentiation and inclusion strategies are being used effectively.

LIST 79 Recording assessment

All good teachers know that teaching is the most effective when it is made a team effort. In order to share your findings with others, you must always make sure that any records you make are clear and concise.

○ Ensure regular assessment reports are made across the whole school and department.
○ Ensure any reports are made accessible to all who may need them.
○ Ensure the assessment report matches the assessment criteria.
○ Keep judgements fair and accurate.
○ Always refer to National Curriculum guidelines if necessary.
○ Keep marking criteria systematic and in a constant format.
○ Share results with your department to ensure potential problems can be approached and dealt with.
○ Keep back-up documents of formal assessments.
○ Use these records to help when designing strategies or setting targets – they will help you plan your teaching goals.
○ Be aware that the records are not just for your use, but for the use of your department, school, educational inspectors and parents – so keep them professional.

LIST 80

Using ICT to record assessment

ICT can help in the collection, recording and presentation of essential data. However, in order to be successful, it is essential this data is both collected and used in the right way.

If used incorrectly, any data stored on a machine can simply become just another filing cabinet, and the benefits of using ICT for assessment are lost. In addition to storing information, teachers can use ICT to help facilitate planning and organizing, to design and store resources and create interactive assessment tools.

It is essential that teachers encourage the use of ICT across the curriculum, and learn how to use it effectively themselves.

Benefits of using ICT in assessment

- Faster and easier to plan, prepare and deliver lesson resources.
- Ability to design and modify assessment records and feedback sheets.
- Implementation of technology into the classroom such as interactive whiteboards or laptop use encourages a variety of ICT skills.
- Current plans by the UK government to implement e-assessment – National Curriculum tests and exams available in electronic format.
- Use of specific software such as MAPS (e-portfolio management tool).
- E-Assessment tools – accurate and searchable record-keeping/ data collection and opportunities for students to do assessment tasks on-screen.
- E-Learning opportunities such as Virtual Learning Environments (VLEs) encourage wider learning.
- Better monitoring and sharing of assessment criteria/records.
- Teachers can be alerted to potential areas of concern faster and can adapt their teaching as necessary.
- Formative and summative assessment strategies can be faster and more frequent.
- Can be used to aid self-assessment – students can work at their own pace.
- Potentially less time spent on marking.

- Recording and calculation of grades in databases or spreadsheets.
- Provision of interactive learning tools such as quizzes, tests, tasks, research requirements, etc.
- Use of intranet or the Internet for research and discovery and to manage ICT-assisted work.
- More practical method of extracting and storing information.
- Reduces the amount of paper resources required.

Potential problems of using ICT in assessment

- Technical failures – files and reports can be lost due to computer/user error.
- Possible impact on face-to-face teacher–student interaction.
- Too reliant on technology – other important skills may be lost.
- Can take a long time to develop or implement initially.
- Changes to the curriculum could mean some assessment strategies are no longer needed.

LIST 81
Reducing the assessment load

All assessment, especially the written kind, takes time. One of the major contributing factors to teacher stress is the workload they have to endure. To cut down on the amount of time you spend on making and recording assessments, try to remember these eight helpful tips.

1. Organize and reduce the amount of assessment needed. Concentrate on key assessment areas and set tasks that are focused on specific areas of assessment.
2. When appropriate, choose assessment tasks that take less time to mark – essays and portfolios take longer to mark than quizzes, tests and multiple-choice tasks.
3. Allocate realistic time to deal with marking and assessment and keep up to date.
4. Use clear marking guides, and give copies to your students – this means you are clear about what to mark and they know what to do to get good marks.
5. Use modelling effectively in your teaching – a student who is clear on what is expected of them will have fewer problems, work more efficiently and produce better work.
6. Take a wider approach to assessment – sometimes it is possible to assess one or two learning objectives in one assignment.
7. Be succinct when making comments – not every piece of marking needs a detailed comment.
8. Delegate your marking – where possible, share large assessment loads with colleagues.

Remember: *saving time is good; laziness is not.*

Never compromise effective teaching and learning strategies just to reduce your marking workload.

Oral Assessment

9

LIST 82   Assessing oral tasks

Oral tasks often seem like the easy assessment option when compared to marking essays or projects, but it is important to remember that they are just as serious a form of assessment.

When setting oral tasks to be assessed, always consider:

○ The exact assessment criteria – ensure you are critiquing how the task has been approached and delivery skills, not the student's actual speaking.

○ How much preparation has been done on this task – speaking and listening tasks are similar to other activities in that they take preparation, practice and some coaching of skills.

○ The purpose of evaluation is to improve performance, not to judge.

○ Give useful and specific feedback that focuses on how to improve as well as assessing the performance: e.g. *'You maintained good eye contact and spoke aloud well, but you constantly fiddled with your script which was distracting to the audience.'*
'You frequently turned your back on the audience, and sometimes it was difficult to hear what you said.'

○ Use both oral and written feedback – writing down your comments means that students can review these before their next performance.

○ Give students the opportunity to evaluate themselves and comment on their performance.

○ When assessing multiple individual or group presentations, it is better to deliver feedback at the end of all the performances to avoid later speakers using 'hints' you may have given earlier speakers.

○ If appropriate, some students may prefer private assessments or videotaping their performances – this can help with any performance anxiety issues, and can be used for further in-depth assessment later on.

Key points for assessing oral ability

It can be much harder to assess the spoken word over the written, as it is almost impossible to go back and check what has been said unless you record the task on audio or visual equipment. When assessing oral ability, you may find it helpful to keep these key points in mind:

- How does the piece of work relate to the objective and outcomes of the task?
- What key points are you looking for as an assessor and how will you assess an oral task?
- Have the students shown evidence that they have followed the discussion?
- Have the students developed ideas and sequenced events through their speaking?
- Does the student show confidence or good speaking ability?
- Does the student show respect for others' views, and has he/she shown they have listened to the opinions and ideas of others?
- Does the student communicate effectively?
- Has the student asked questions to develop ideas?
- If required, do the students respond to questions as well as their own opinions?
- Is the student's vocabulary and attitude appropriate and do they adapt it if necessary according to the situation?
- Has the student used appropriate language, vocabulary and terminology, e.g. Standard English, slang, French, etc.?
- Has the student engaged, and shown an awareness of, the audience through their use of tone, pace and style?
- Is there evidence that the student can judge when to lead and participate in a discussion and when to encourage others to participate?
- Is the student a confident, articulate and perceptive speaker and listener?

Ideas for oral assessment

While many of these tasks will be used automatically throughout English and Drama sessions, they are to be encouraged in other subjects too.

Remember: Plenary sessions are also an excellent way of assessing oral ability and understanding.

Talk about and discuss

○ Plays, poetry and novels
○ Non-fiction texts
○ Personal experiences:
  e.g. *A memorable day*
  A school trip to a museum
  My earliest memory
○ New, unfamiliar and sometimes imaginary topics:
  e.g. *Hitler and World War II*
  The day I nearly died
  What I think about crime

Types of tasks

○ Asking and answering questions in class
○ Informal discussions in pairs
○ Informal discussions in groups
○ Giving a talk (formal or informal) to a group or the class
○ Prepared presentations
○ Explaining a report to a group or the class
○ Formal debates
○ Formal paired/group interviews on a specific topic
○ Reading aloud to a small group or the class
○ Role play or drama activities

Effective plenary sessions

A plenary is the last part of a four-part lesson structure. Many teachers seem to forget their importance, and the positive impact they can have on their lessons.

A plenary can be as simple as a 5-minute oral summary of the lesson, and acts not only to 'wind down' the lesson, but also to recap the aims and objectives covered.

The aim of a plenary is to

- ○ Pull the whole group together at the end of the lesson.
- ○ Summarize the level of learning that has taken place so far.
- ○ Consolidate the learning.
- ○ Lead on to the next stage of learning.
- ○ Help determine the next steps for learning.

The purpose of a plenary is to

- ○ Help pupils understand and remember what they have learned.
- ○ Refer back to the learning objectives in the starter.
- ○ Create a sense of achievement, gain and completion.
- ○ Simply evaluate what level the class has reached that lesson.
- ○ Help take learning further.

A plenary helps teachers by

- ○ Encouraging students to reflect on their learning.
- ○ Helping pupils to communicate about what they have learned.
- ○ Helping to encourage interest, and curiosity about the next stage of learning.
- ○ Acting as a form of summative assessment.
- ○ Acting as a diagnostic tool to determine how well the class has progressed and achieved, and what the next step of learning should be.

- ○ Useful phrases for an oral plenary session include:
  'Can anyone tell me what we have learned today?'
  'What was the objective of this lesson?'
  'Give me three key words that we have learned in this lesson today.'
  'Can you explain/tell me how … [e.g. mathematical formula, science result, spelling of word etc.].'

○ Useful plenary ideas also include:
  – List three new things you have learnt today.
  – Write all the words relating to today's work that you can remember in one minute.
  – Think of a mnemonic to help you remember today's key themes.
  – Draw a diagram or picture to help you remember today's key themes.
  – What do you think we will learn next? / What do you think we will study next?
  – Quick-fire test: spelling, true or false, mathematical answers, scientific element quiz, etc.

Useful comments for assessing oral presentations

The three-rule marking strategy of 'A Star, A Rainbow and A Wish' can also be appropriate for making oral assessments.

Always take care when making any comments; always be fair and appraising. Just because a comment is not written down for all posterity, does not mean it might not come back to haunt you!

○ Comments should show which areas the student did well in as well as the areas they were weak in:
'You spoke very clearly and confidently, but you failed to make eye-contact with the audience.'

○ Comments should be positive, praising and encouraging:
'Well done.'
'A lovely presentation.'

○ Comments should be informative and easy to understand:
'You spoke well about the subject material and you clearly understood the task.'
'You engaged the audience and kept them entertained while being informative and confident.'

○ Comments should encourage the student in ways to improve:
'Next time you may find it useful to use prompt cards rather than reading from a script.'
'When we do this again, I would like to see you really using your voice and speaking a bit louder so we can all hear you.'

○ Always support your comments with evidence:
'I did not see you interact very well with the other members of your group, and sometimes you did not listen to what they were telling you.'
'You did not engage the complete audience as you kept your eyes on the right hand side of the room.'

○ Ensure your comments build confidence and self-esteem – remember that speaking aloud can be very nerve-wracking for many students:
'I could see that you were very nervous about this task, but you have performed very well indeed, and you should be very proud of yourself.'

○ Encourage other students to be supportive of others' achievements:

'Let's all give Samantha a big round of applause.'

○ Keep oral work focused:

e.g. when a student gets the giggles or misbehaves during a presentation.

'I understand that you are nervous, but you need to take a deep breath and focus on your performance now.'

'Unfortunately your behaviour is going to lose you marks and I want you to be focused and sensible.'

Written Assessment 10

Assessing and promoting literacy – cross-curriculum

To help promote a good use and understanding of English, the UK government introduced the National Literacy Strategy. The aim is to promote literacy across the school and to improve national literacy results.

Results have shown that pupils with a good command of literacy also achieve higher grades in other subjects.

Remember: promoting literacy is not just for English teachers!

○ Effective literacy is flexible, dynamic and constantly developed.
○ Literacy is not just about the written or spoken word, it also includes understanding numbers, symbols and data.
○ Equate literacy skills with communication skills:
  – learning through conversing (speaking/listening)
  – learning through reading/text
  – learning through writing
○ Encourage proper use of spelling, punctuation and grammar in all written work.
○ Display key words and phrases on the board or around the room.
○ Take care over your own spelling, punctuation and grammar.
○ Encourage written exercises in all subjects.

LIST 88 Ideas for assessing literacy: subject-based

[Note: The following ideas are not necessarily subject-specific and can also be attributed to many other curriculum areas.]

English

Reading skills – e.g. close reading, proof reading, skim/scan reading, reading aloud, etc.; research skills; speaking and listening exercises; individual and group presentations; reporting and presenting information in a variety of formats; spelling, punctuation and grammar skills; improving communication; understanding texts; critical analysis and transformation of texts; understanding of style, format, tone, audience, etc.; inquiry skills; reflective thinking; exploring media; creative writing skills; exploring historical literature; oral tasks; group work and communication skills.

Mathematics

Explaining or solving logical problems; presenting and interpreting solutions to a problem; speaking and listening exercises; exploring mathematical concepts; understanding mathematical syntax; using tables, diagrams and charts; close reading to interpret information in a variety of formats; research of historical mathematical movements.

Sciences

Writing up experiments accurately; close study of a specific topic; designing posters and articles to explain scientific processes; writing scientific reports; understanding key words in science; understanding and interpreting information and statistics; understanding scientific syntax and vocabulary; assessing how scientific text is presented in articles and newspapers.

Modern Foreign Languages

Translation exercises; writing letters or articles; creating posters and articles; understanding and application of grammar in both English and the target language; use of dictionaries; understanding of how language works through analysis; pronunciation and spelling of English and target language; conversing in and understanding other languages.

ICT

Understanding context as well as structure through presentation, discussion and analysis of textual examples; text frames for group work; editing and formatting text; preparation and presentation of information in different formats; understanding technical terms; research skills; creating newspaper articles or advertisements; understanding punctuation or lexis; spell checking and thesaurus exercises; exploring the Internet; using mind-mapping software.

Physical Education

Communicating and expressing shape and form; expressing fundamental targets of PE and physical health; word or spelling throwing-and-catching games; research and study skills in areas of health and PE; discussion exercises to help explain and understand the key aims of health and physical fitness; planning and evaluating sequences; mind-mapping ideas.

Humanities

Investigating and reporting information in written or oral format; extracting and organizing information; interpreting different types of text and data such as maps or historical texts; using encyclopaedias, atlases and the media; using and understanding specific terminology; creating posters, maps, articles or presentations to share knowledge and understanding.

Art and Design Technology

Understanding historical art movements; researching designs and processes; presenting information in charts, diagrams or images; creating and following instructions; planning and preparing information; discussing techniques and ideas; evaluating artistic progress; exploring design properties of materials; creating and performing presentations; assessing and evaluating progress and final pieces.

Drama and Media

Reading and writing scripts; organizing sequences or techniques; explaining form and shape and dramatic impact; analysing performance; speaking to large audiences; understanding specific terminology; communicating feelings and emotions; planning and evaluating performances; using the media; exploring media techniques and their impact; understanding and explaining narrative.

Citizenship and PSHE

Understanding other cultures and ethnicities; explaining and understanding political and cultural differences; exploring contemporary issues; discussing and expressing ideas; exploring and understanding the media (television, newspapers, Internet), and their influence; encouraging involvement in community issues; exploring and understanding the values of citizenship; understanding human rights; researching historical ideas regarding citizenship; group discussions and presentations on key areas; exploring other religions and faiths.

L I S T 89   Assessing writing ability

○ How does the piece of work relate to the objective and outcomes of the task?

○ What key points are you looking for as an assessor?

○ How has the student demonstrated a sound grasp of the task?

○ Consider the student's use of spelling, punctuation and grammar – is this accurate or appropriate to the task?

○ How is the work presented:
  - is the writing legible?
  - has the student used cursive or printed handwriting?
  - is there a clear use of paragraphing?
  - if appropriate, has the student used ICT effectively?

○ Is the style and vocabulary used appropriate to the task?

○ Is the work original – is there clear evidence that this is the student's own work?

○ Are there any contributing factors that may have an impact on how the student has completed this task? e.g. SEN, ESOL, G&T, age, gender, etc.

○ Is there clear evidence to show good progression in the student's work?

○ Is there evidence that shows the pupils have understood the outcomes expected and/or made an active attempt to direct their writing to fulfil the set criteria?

○ If appropriate, how does the work compare to the work of those of a similar age, gender, peer group, etc.?

L I S T 90

Useful comments for assessing written work

○ Comments should help the student see what they got right and understand where they have gone wrong:
  'You made an excellent start but forgot to ...'

○ Comments should be positive, praising and encouraging:
  'Well done.'
  'This is super work.'
  'You have made an excellent effort.'

○ Comments should offer suggestions on how to solve a problem, not give away the answer when the student is stuck.
  'Look carefully at your working out and see if you can spot where you have made any errors.'

○ Comments should be clear and explicit:
  'I can see you have found this task hard. We will work together and find a way to help you improve.'

○ Comments should help the student to learn and improve:
  'You will find page ... in your textbook helpful with this work.'
  'We have covered this topic in an earlier class, you may find it helpful to look through your classnotes.'

○ When commenting on presentation, avoid being negative but point out the poor presentation skills:
  'Be careful with your handwriting. You risk losing marks in an exam if you have poor presentation. Try leaving more space and increase the size of your writing.'

○ Use comments to refer back to other areas that the student has covered:
  'You are still making the same errors that you have made before. Please read my marking carefully to see where you have gone wrong.'

○ Never use comments such as *'Rubbish!'* or *'You must try harder'* as they will only discourage the student.

LIST 91 Useful marking symbols for written work

The following are the most commonly used marking symbols for assessing written work.

Be aware, however, many teachers, departments and schools have their own marking systems, and as long as your marking stays systematic you may find you develop your own symbols.

/ /	Begin or insert new paragraph
/	Leave a space here
P	Punctuation is incorrect (some teachers also circle wrong punctuation)
?	Unclear or does not make sense
∧	Word or letter missing
___	(Underlined) Word used or section is incorrect
Sp.	Spelling is incorrect (many teachers just circle misspellings)
~	Incorrect grammar used (it is helpful to annotate this kind of mistake with exactly what kind of grammatical error has been made, e.g. *tense*)
---	(Lines through words) Delete this section
~~	Curvy line through or under words – space not needed
→	Indent this section
✓	Good Work
✓✓	Very good work
✗	Incorrect
Cap.	Capitalize
LC	Use lower case
W	Write the word out in full – don't use an abbreviation or symbol
Rep.	Repetition/repeated word

Writing reports

As part of your teaching duties you will be expected to write end of term and end of year reports that will be taken home and shown to parents and guardians.

Simple rules for report writing

- Keep comments positive and refer to achievements.
- Avoid generalizations – be specific and concise.
- Do not refer to the students' personality – focus more on their academic progress.
- Offer ways to improve or progress rather than criticize.
- Always be honest and fair.
- Take your time over content and presentation.
- Remember that many parents are very protective of their little darlings! Steer well clear of jokes, ambiguity or sarcasm – always be professional.

Words to avoid

These might seem obvious, but sometimes words like these do slip in even unintentionally:

thick, stupid, bad, rude, silly, annoying, troublesome, difficult, idiot, appalling, slow, devious, sly, trouble-maker, bully, awkward, retarded, dim, pathetic, rubbish.

20 useful phrases for report cards

Remember: Keep reports positive and truthful. If you can't find anything nice to say, don't say anything at all!

1. *Has performed very well in ...*
2. *Has an excellent attitude/good temperament.*
3. *Is highly motivated/responsible.*
4. *Is pleasant and helpful.*
5. *Has made considerable improvement in ...*
6. *Is an excellent team player./Works well with others.*
7. *Has worked very hard in ...*
8. *Shows a lot of promise.*
9. *Shows real interest and enthusiasm.*
10. *Is consistently progressing in ...*
11. *Is a conscientious worker.*
12. *Is mature and reliable/is especially confident in ...*
13. *Follows directions/instructions well.*
14. *Has made a real contribution to ...*
15. *Participates well in conversation and discussion work.*
16. *Shows a positive attitude to learning.*
17. *Is independent/self-reliant.*
18. *Is eager to learn/concentrates well.*
19. *Is organized/efficient/driven to succeed.*
20. *Is particularly creative/shows real originality/clarity of thinking.*

What not to write on the report card!

No matter how tempting it may be to use some of these, remember, these are just for laughs!

1. Since my last report, your child has hit rock bottom and has started to dig.
2. I would not allow this student to breed.
3. Your child has delusions of adequacy.
4. Your child is depriving a village of an idiot.
5. Your child sets low personal standards and then consistently fails to achieve them.
6. This child has been working with glue too much.
7. When your son's IQ reaches 50, he should sell.
8. The lights are on but no one is home.
9. If your child were any dumber, they would have to be watered twice a week.
10. It is impossible to believe the sperm that created this child beat 1,000,000 others.

Teacher Assessment | **11**

LIST 95 — Becoming the best

I hear and I forget,
I see and I remember,
I do and I understand.
    Confucius *c.* 450 BC

Just as assessment is a cyclical process, so too is teaching and learning. Good teachers will also be good learners and will seek to develop their teaching methods in order to improve and expand their teaching skills.

Sometimes it is not enough to be a *good* teacher, you want to be a *great* one. The following are very simple steps you can take to become the best teacher you can.

- Identify and understand different learning styles.
- Find your own learning styles and adapt your approaches to teaching and learning.
- Take an active approach to your career.
- Engage in constant self and peer appraisal.
- Consider professional development training.
- Make the most of your skills and identify weaknesses to improve.
- Consider how you want your career to develop.
- Teach and learn collaboratively: teaching is teamwork – be an active part of your department.
- Manage your time effectively.
- It is not important to know all the answers, but it is important to know where to look for them.
- Cooperate and communicate.
- Be patient, enthusiastic and keep a good sense of humour.
- Plan flexibly but rigorously – always seek to improve your subject knowledge.
- Enjoy your work!

The iceberg theory

A good teacher is ...?

10 per cent classroom practice

90 per cent evaluation, routine
preparation, planning,
professional judgement,
subject knowledge, pedagogical knowledge, personality

Self-assessment for teachers

It's not just students who suffer from low self-esteem; sometimes teachers do too. If you feel that you are having problems, never be afraid to ask for help. Taking time to do some self-assessment may help you realize which areas you need to address, develop and even change.

- ❍ Determine which areas you feel you need to improve in: planning, prioritizing, behaviour management, etc.
- ❍ Devise an action plan to assist you when working on these areas.
- ❍ Prioritize your duties – plan effectively and efficiently.
- ❍ Make good use of your Planning, Preparation and Assessment (PPA) time. Ensure you are getting the statutory 10 per cent non-contact time.
- ❍ Enquire about professional development courses and further training to improve your skills.
- ❍ Take full advantage of Teacher Training Days and Personal Development Days.
- ❍ Consider the use of a teaching portfolio to document your career progression.
- ❍ Keep a teaching journal to reflect on your teaching. Record both good and bad lessons and try to determine if there are any patterns.
- ❍ Work with your department and other members of staff to help work through problem areas – remember teaching is teamwork.
- ❍ Consider team teaching with other members of staff.
- ❍ Observe more experienced members of staff to see how they approach problem areas and to share skills.
- ❍ Get other members of staff to observe you and comment on your skills and weaknesses.
- ❍ Record one of your teaching sessions on a videotape or cassette and review it later – this allows you to see your teaching from another angle and may help you spot problem areas more easily.
- ❍ Ask your students' opinion: what do they think of your teaching? This could be through the use of a questionnaire or class discussion.
- ❍ Involve the students in your planning – this may help you to plan more effective lessons and engage your classes.

○ Discuss any problems or areas of concern with colleagues, other professional educators or union representatives – don't try to struggle through problems on your own.

LIST 97   What makes a good teacher?

Everyone has a different idea about what makes a truly good teacher. Effective teaching is not just about what you know but how you communicate it. Your personality, communication skills and pedagogy are all important factors towards being an excellent teacher, not just your subject knowledge.

Remember: everyone is different, and all teachers are different. Part of becoming a good teacher is finding out what works for you by constantly assessing your skills.

Some key defining factors of a good teacher include:

○ A genuine enjoyment of their work.
○ A genuine interest in helping their students.
○ The ability to make learning fun and enjoyable.
○ A high level of understanding and respect for all students.
○ High expectations of all students.
○ Drive, ambition and a good sense of purpose.
○ An ability to learn as well as teach.
○ A willingness to change and adapt as necessary.
○ Good understanding of the need for assessment and personal reflection.
○ Excellent organization, planning and time-management skills.
○ The ability to work well within a team as well as independently.
○ Actively involving students in their learning.

Observing other teachers

Some teachers make teaching look so easy!

It is not just trainees and NQTs who should participate in observations.

Taking the time to observe other teachers to watch how they teach is an excellent way of improving your own skills (and identifying where you might be going wrong!).

Useful points to consider when observing

○ Professional values, practice and attitude:
   How do they enter the room? Are they friendly or serious? Do they appear relaxed or focused? Do they have a good relationship with the class?

○ Knowledge and understanding of subject area:
   Do they have sound subject knowledge? Do they refer to notes? How do they show and share their knowledge?

○ Effective use of resources, equipment and space:
   Do they use textbooks or handouts? How is the classroom laid out? Do they use OHPs or ICT?

○ Planning, aims, expectations and target setting:
   Are the objectives/outcomes clearly explained? Do they have high expectations of the class? How do they approach the lesson?

○ Use of monitoring and assessment:
   Are books marked and up to date? Do they praise good behaviour consistently? Do they monitor how the lesson progresses?

○ Class/behaviour management techniques:
   Do they deal with unwanted behaviour quickly and efficiently? How do they keep command of the class? Do they use any unusual or different methods to keep the class on-task?

○ Interaction with class, pacing and time-keeping:
   Is the lesson well paced? Do they use the time effectively? How do they keep the class focused? Do they engage the class well?

○ Teaching style/methods used:
   Do they talk a lot or use visual resources? Do they use group work or encourage individual learning? How do they promote positive learning?

○ Any obvious strengths and weaknesses:
   Is the lesson interesting and engaging? Have they planned well? Do they stick to the four-part lesson plan?
○ Summary of observation:
   How did the lesson go overall? Were the aims and objectives achieved? Did the class progress well? Was this a successful lesson?

LIST 99   QTS standards

In order to achieve Qualified Teacher Status from the General Teaching Council, all trainee teachers must achieve all of the 42 standards set by the Teacher Training Agency (TTA).

However, to constantly improve your teaching ability, even fully qualified and experienced teachers can assess their own skills against these criteria.

The following abridged standards list can be used to ensure your teaching and assessment skills are of excellent quality.

[Note: The full standards document can be found on the Teacher Training Agency website: www.tta.gov.uk]

Teaching, monitoring and assessment, and class management

3.1.1 Set challenging teaching and learning objectives relevant to all pupils.
3.1.2 Good use of T&L objectives to plan and assess lessons.
3.1.3 Selection and preparation of relevant resources.
3.1.4 Involved in, and contribute to, teaching teams.
3.1.5 Provide opportunities for out-of-school learning activities.
3.2.1 Appropriate use of monitoring and assessment strategies.
3.2.2 Monitor and assess as they teach.
3.2.3 Accurate assessment of pupil progress with regard to national criteria.
3.2.4 Identify and support more and less able students (SEN, G&T, etc.).
3.2.5 Identify and support EAL students.
3.2.6 Record pupils' progress and achievements accurately and consistently.
3.2.7 Communicate pupils' progress and assessment for parents, other professionals and pupils.
3.3.1 High expectations of pupils' teaching and learning.
3.3.2 Teach appropriate and engaging lessons to the age range they are trained to teach.
3.3.3 Teach structured lessons and sequences of work, which engage, interest and motivate students, and have clear learning objectives.

3.3.4   Differentiate teaching to meet all pupils' needs.

3.3.5   Support EAL students.

3.3.6   Understand how gender, culture and ethnicity can affect learning ability and contribute to students' needs.

3.3.7   Good organization and time management of teaching and learning.

3.3.8   Good organization of physical teaching space, with good regard of health and safety.

3.3.9   Manage and control pupil behaviour through clear frameworks.

3.3.10   Use ICT effectively.

3.3.11   Teach over a sustained period of time.

3.3.12   Provide relevant homework to promote effective autonomous learning.

3.3.13   Work effectively with other teachers and education professionals.

3.3.14   Promote equal opportunities within the school.

Teaching portfolios

All teachers can benefit from the use of a teaching portfolio at any point in their career. It is not just trainee teachers and NQTs that should document their skills; even experienced teachers gain rewards through self-assessment.

A teaching portfolio should document your skills and achievements and allow you to see how your career has progressed. Portfolios can also increase your job prospects and help you become aware of any areas for improvement.

Things to include

- Teaching responsibilities: describe courses taught, numbers of students, age range and level of ability. Any specialist skills can also be documented here.
- Teaching philosophy: knowledge of pedagogy and subject area. Describe your teaching beliefs and your view of education. The goals you have set for yourself and your students. How you see your career progressing.
- Products of teaching and/or evidence of learning: course planning and preparation, examples of graded work, student evaluation and feedback. You might also include effective examples of your teaching and the methods you used.
- Teaching evaluations: observations from other members of staff, student feedback, feedback from colleagues. Self-assessment and personal achievements.
- Efforts to improve your teaching: documentation of teaching development courses or workshops, contributions to the school or department, curriculum revisions you may have made, self or peer assessment documentation, steps you have taken to evaluate and improve your teaching and learning.
- Additional qualifications achieved.
- Other items: self-evaluations of teaching-related areas, references, commendations, contributions to educational publications, evidence of assisting other teachers/trainees.

Templates for assessment

Creating assessment records and marking grids

This template can be adapted for any subject, ability and age.

The number of objectives and levels included can be adapted to suit the assessment range as required.

As well as finding this template useful as a marking guide, teachers can work through each objective and tick off the level as a student has attained it. It not only makes marking easier and faster, but also can be used as a feedback form for the student allowing them to assess their own attainment at a glance.

Simple example

Assessment Record (Subject)				
Name of student Date			Class Assessor	
	Level 1	Level 2	Level 3	Level 4
Objectives to be achieved (as many as required) ↓	Description of identifiable performance characteristics Basic Level	Description of identifiable performance characteristics Development Level	Description of identifiable performance characteristics Competent Level	Description of identifiable performance characteristics Master Level
Total / further comments				

Complex Example

Assessment Record / Marking Grid (Subject)				
Name of student Date of assessment			Class/Subject Assessor	
Level ↓	Objective/ identifiable performance criteria	Objective/ identifiable performance criteria	Objective/ identifiable performance criteria	Objective/ identifiable performance criteria
Level 1	Basic level criteria			→
Level 2	Development level criteria			→
Level 3	Competent level criteria			→
Level 4	Master level criteria			→
Above Level 4	Exceptional performance			→

Comments	
Level	[ ]

Outer Threshold				
Below Level 1	Very basic criteria			→
	↓			
Above Level 4	Exceptional performance			→

Assessing oral work

Oral work can be particularly awkward to assess, as it can be difficult to make detailed assessment notes while paying close attention to the presentation. This example template can be adapted for use in a wide range of subjects and allows the teacher to tick or mark objectives as they are achieved. It can also be used as evidence when providing feedback.

Evaluation of an Oral Presentation

Name

	Very good (3)	Satisfactory (2)	Poor (1)
Provided an interesting introduction and gave a clear explanation of the topic.			
Presented the information in a structured order.			
Spoke clearly and confidently in an acceptable manner.			
Used technical terminology/ linguistic techniques appropriately.			
Maintained eye contact and used correct body language			
Showed evidence of understanding the topic / prior preparation / research			
Summarised or concluded the presentation satisfactorily.			
Engaged and sustained audience interest.			
Answered questions/ comments from the audience well.			
Used any presentation aids satisfactorily (audio/visual/ ICT)			

Total _____ (out of 30)

Any further comments

Student self-assessment record

This self-assessment form can be used to help students take an active role in their learning and assessment.

It encourages them to think about their skills and weaknesses and how they might improve.

Student Self-Assessment Record	
Name Date	Subject
Brief explanation of the task you have done.	
What do you think you did well? State why.	
What do you think you could have improved on? State why.	
If you had the chance to do this task again, what do you think you would change? State why.	
Overall, how do you rate your performance in this task? State why.	
Any other comments you would like to add:	
Teacher comments Score	

Teacher observation form

Classroom Observation Form	
Name of teacher observed	Name of observer
Date Time	Class Topic

Professional values and attitude

Knowledge and understanding of topic

Planning, target setting and expectations

Monitoring and assessment practices

Teaching, behaviour and class management

Summary / any additional comments